St. Louis Community College

Library

5801 Wilson Avenue
St. Louis, Missouri 63110

 PRINTED IN U.S.A.

23-263-002

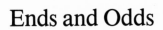

Ends and Odds

Ends and Odds

Eight New Dramatic Pieces

by Samuel Beckett

Grove Press, Inc.
New York

ISBN: 0-394-17918-8
Grove Press ISBN: 0-8021-4028-9

Library of Congress Catalog Card Number: 76-14510

First Evergreen Edition 1976

First Printing

Manufactured in the United States of America

Distributed by Random House, Inc., New York

GROVE PRESS, INC., 196 West Houston Street, New York, N.Y. 10014

ENDS

ODDS

Roughs for Theatre and Radio:

Ends

Not I

Not I

The world premiere of *Not I* was given at the Repertory
Theater of Lincoln Center in New York City on December 7,
1972. It was directed by Alan Schneider, and the settings
were by Douglas W. Schmidt. The cast was as follows:

MOUTH   Jessica Tandy
AUDITOR   Henderson Forsythe

NOTE

Movement: this consists in simple sideways raising of arms from sides and their falling back, in a gesture of helpless compassion. It lessens with each recurrence till scarcely perceptible at third. There is just enough pause to contain it as MOUTH recovers from vehement refusal to relinquish third person.

Stage in darkness but for MOUTH, *upstage audience right, about 8' above stage level, faintly lit from close-up and below, rest of face in shadow. Invisible microphone.* AUDITOR, *downstage audience left, tall standing figure, sex undeterminable, enveloped from head to foot in loose black djellaba, with hood, fully faintly lit, standing on invisible podium about 4' high, shown by attitude alone to be facing diagonally across stage intent on* MOUTH, *dead still throughout but for four brief movements where indicated. See* NOTE.

As house lights down MOUTH'*s voice unintelligible behind curtain. House lights out. Voice continues unintelligible behind curtain, 10 seconds. With rise of curtain ad-libbing from text as required leading when curtain fully up and attention sufficient into:*

MOUTH: . . . out . . . into this world . . . this world . . . tiny little thing . . . before its time . . . in a godfor- . . . what? . . . girl? . . . yes . . . tiny little girl . . . into this . . . out into this . . . before her time . . . godforsaken hole called . . .

[14]

called . . . no matter . . . parents unknown . . . unheard of
. . . he having vanished . . . thin air . . . no sooner buttoned
up his breeches . . . she similarly . . . eight months later . . .
almost to the tick . . . so no love . . . spared that . . . no
love such as normally vented on the . . . speechless infant
. . . in the home . . . no . . . nor indeed for that matter any
of any kind . . . no love of any kind . . . at any subsequent
stage . . . so typical affair . . . nothing of any note till
coming up to sixty when— . . . what? . . . seventy? . . .
good God! . . . coming up to seventy . . . wandering in a
field . . . looking aimlessly for cowslips . . . to make a ball
. . . a few steps then stop . . . stare into space . . . then on
. . . a few more . . . stop and stare again . . . so on . . .
drifting around . . . when suddenly . . . gradually . . . all
went out . . . all that early April morning light . . . and she
found herself in the— . . . what? . . . who? . . . no! . . . she!
. . . (*pause and movement 1*) . . . found herself in the dark
. . . and if not exactly . . . insentient . . . insentient . . . for
she could still hear the buzzing . . . so-called . . . in the ears
. . . and a ray of light came and went . . . came and went
. . . such as the moon might cast . . . drifting . . . in and out
of cloud . . . but so dulled . . . feeling . . . feeling so dulled
. . . she did not know . . . what position she was in . . .
imagine! . . . what position she was in! . . . whether
standing . . . or sitting . . . but the brain— . . . what? . . .
kneeling? . . . yes . . . whether standing . . . or sitting . . . or
kneeling . . . but the brain— . . . what? . . . lying? . . . yes
. . . whether standing . . . or sitting . . . or kneeling . . . or
lying . . . but the brain still . . . in a way . . . for her first
thought was . . . oh long after . . . sudden flash . . . brought
up as she had been to believe . . . with the other waifs . . .

in a merciful ... (*brief laugh*) ... God ... (*good laugh*)
... first thought was ... oh long after ... sudden flash ...
she was being punished ... for her sins ... a number of
which then ... further proof if proof were needed ...
flashed through her mind ... one after another ... then
dismissed as foolish ... oh long after ... this thought
dismissed ... as she suddenly realized ... gradually
realized ... she was not suffering ... imagine! ... not
suffering! ... indeed could not remember ... off-hand ...
when she had suffered less ... unless of course she was ...
meant to be suffering ... ha! ... *thought* to be suffering
... just as the odd time ... in her life ... when clearly
intended to be having pleasure ... she was in fact ...
having none ... not the slightest ... in which case of
course ... that notion of punishment ... for some sin or
other ... or for the lot ... or no particular reason ... for
its own sake ... thing she understood perfectly ... that
notion of punishment ... which had first occurred to her
... brought up as she had been to believe ... with the
other waifs ... in a merciful ... (*brief laugh*) ... God ...
(*good laugh*) ... first occurred to her ... then dismissed
... as foolish ... was perhaps not so foolish ... after all
... so on ... all that ... vain reasonings ... till another
thought ... oh long after ... sudden flash ... very foolish
really but— ... what? ... the buzzing? ... yes ... all the
time the buzzing ... so-called ... in the ears ... though of
course actually ... not in the ears at all ... in the skull ...
dull roar in the skull ... and all the time this ray or beam
... like moonbeam ... but probably not ... certainly not
... always the same spot ... now bright ... now shrouded
... but always the same spot ... as no moon could ... no

. . . no moon . . . just all part of the same wish to . . . torment . . . though actually in point of fact . . . not in the least . . . not a twinge . . . so far . . . ha! . . . so far . . . this other thought then . . . oh long after . . . sudden flash . . . very foolish really but so like her . . . in a way . . . that she might do well to . . . groan . . . on and off . . . writhe she could not . . . as if in actual . . . agony . . . but could not . . . could not bring herself . . . some flaw in her make-up . . . incapable of deceit . . . or the machine . . . more likely the machine . . . so disconnected . . . never got the message . . . or powerless to respond . . . like numbed . . . couldn't make the sound . . . not any sound . . . no sound of any kind . . . no screaming for help for example . . . should she feel so inclined . . . scream . . . (*screams*) . . . then listen . . . (*silence*) . . . scream again . . . (*screams again*) . . . then listen again . . . (*silence*) . . . no . . . spared that . . . all silent as the grave . . . no part— . . . what? . . . the buzzing? . . . yes . . . all silent but for the buzzing . . . so-called . . . no part of her moving . . . that she could feel . . . just the eyelids . . . presumably . . . on and off . . . shut out the light . . . reflex they call it . . . no feeling of any kind . . . but the lids . . . even best of times . . . who feels them? . . . opening . . . shutting . . . all that moisture . . . but the brain still . . . still sufficiently . . . oh very much so! . . . at this stage . . . in control . . . under control . . . to question even this . . . for on that April morning . . . so it reasoned . . . that April morning . . . she fixing with her eye . . . a distant bell . . . as she hastened towards it . . . fixing it with her eye . . . lest it elude her . . . had not all gone out . . . all that light . . . of itself . . . without any . . . any . . . on her

Ends and Odds

part . . . so on . . . so on it reasoned . . . vain questionings
. . . and all dead still . . . sweet silent as the grave . . . when
suddenly . . . gradually . . . she realiz– . . . what? . . . the
buzzing? . . . yes . . . all dead still but for the buzzing . . .
when suddenly she realized . . . words were– . . . what? . . .
who? . . . no! . . . she! . . . (*pause and movement 2*) . . . realized . . . words were coming . . . imagine! . . . words were coming . . . a voice she did not recognize . . . at first . . . so long
since it had sounded . . . then finally had to admit . . . could
be none other . . . than her own . . . certain vowel sounds . . .
she had never heard . . . elsewhere . . . so that people would
stare . . . the rare occasions . . . once or twice a year . . .
always winter some strange reason . . . stare at her
uncomprehending . . . and now this stream . . . steady
stream . . . she who had never . . . on the contrary . . .
practically speechless . . . all her days . . . how she
survived! . . . even shopping . . . out shopping . . . busy
shopping centre . . . supermart . . . just hand in the list . . .
with the bag . . . old black shopping bag . . . then stand
there waiting . . . any length of time . . . middle of the
throng . . . motionless . . . staring into space . . . mouth
half open as usual . . . till it was back in her hand . . .
the bag back in her hand . . . then pay and go . . . not
as much as goodbye . . . how she survived! . . . and now
this stream . . . not catching the half of it . . . not the
quarter . . . no idea . . . what she was saying . . . imagine!
. . . no idea what she was saying! . . . till she began
trying to . . . delude herself . . . it was not hers at all
. . . not her voice at all . . . and no doubt would have . . .
vital she should . . . was on the point . . . after long efforts
. . . when suddenly she felt . . . gradually she felt . . . her

[18]

lips moving . . . imagine! . . . her lips moving! . . . as of
course till then she had not . . . and not alone the lips . . .
the cheeks . . . the jaws . . . the whole face . . . all those—
. . . what? . . . the tongue? . . . yes . . . the tongue in the
mouth . . . all those contortions without which . . . no
speech possible . . . and yet in the ordinary way . . . not
felt at all . . . so intent one is . . . on what one is saying . . .
the whole being . . . hanging on its words . . . so that not
only she had . . . had she . . . not only had she . . . to give
up . . . admit hers alone . . . her voice alone . . . but this
other awful thought . . . oh long after . . . sudden flash . . .
even more awful if possible . . . that feeling was coming
back . . . imagine! . . . feeling coming back! . . . starting at
the top . . . then working down . . . the whole machine . . .
but no . . . spared that . . . the mouth alone . . . so far . . .
ha! . . . so far . . . then thinking . . . oh long after . . .
sudden flash . . . it can't go on . . . all this . . . all that . . .
steady stream . . . straining to hear . . . make something of
it . . . and her own thoughts . . . make something of them
. . . all— . . . what? . . . the buzzing? . . . yes . . . all the time
the buzzing . . . so-called . . . all that together . . . imagine!
. . . whole body like gone . . . just the mouth . . . lips . . .
cheeks . . . jaws . . . never— . . . what? . . . tongue? . . . yes
. . . lips . . . cheeks . . . jaws . . . tongue . . . never still a
second . . . mouth on fire . . . stream of words . . . in her
ear . . . practically in her ear . . . not catching the half . . .
not the quarter . . . no idea what she's saying! . . . imagine!
. . . no idea what she's saying! . . . and can't stop . . . no
stopping it . . . she who but a moment before . . . but a
moment! . . . could not make a sound . . . no sound of any
kind . . . now can't stop . . . imagine! . . . can't stop the

stream . . . and the whole brain begging . . . something begging in the brain . . . begging the mouth to stop . . . pause a moment . . . if only for a moment . . . and no response . . . as if it hadn't heard . . . or couldn't . . . couldn't pause a second . . . like maddened . . . all that together . . . straining to hear . . . piece it together . . . and the brain . . . raving away on its own . . . trying to make sense of it . . . or make it stop . . . or in the past . . . dragging up the past . . . flashes from all over . . . walks mostly . . . walking all her days . . . day after day . . . a few steps then stop . . . stare into space . . . then on . . . a few more . . . stop and stare again . . . so on . . . drifting around . . . day after day . . . or that time she cried . . . the one time she could remember . . . since she was a baby . . . must have cried as a baby . . . perhaps not . . . not essential to life . . . just the birth cry to get her going . . . breathing . . . then no more till this . . . old hag already . . . sitting staring at her hand . . . where was it? . . . Croker's Acres . . . one evening on the way home . . . home! . . . a little mound in Croker's Acres . . . dusk . . . sitting staring at her hand . . . there in her lap . . . palm upward . . . suddenly saw it wet . . . the palm . . . tears presumably . . . hers presumably . . . no one else for miles . . . no sound . . . just the tears . . . sat and watched them dry . . . all over in a second . . . or grabbing at the straw . . . the brain . . . flickering away on its own . . . quick grab and on . . . nothing there . . . on to the next . . . bad as the voice . . . worse . . . as little sense . . . all that together . . . can't— . . . what? . . . the buzzing . . . yes . . . all the time the buzzing . . . dull roar like falls . . . and the beam . . . flickering on and off . . . starting to move around . . . like moonbeam

but not . . . all part of the same . . . keep an eye on that
too . . . corner of the eye . . . all that together . . . can't go
on . . . God is love . . . she'll be purged . . . back in the field
. . . morning sun . . . April . . . sink face down in the grass . . .
nothing but the larks . . . so on . . . grabbing at the straw
. . . straining to hear . . . the odd word . . . make some
sense of it . . . whole body like gone . . . just the mouth . . .
like maddened . . . and can't stop . . . no stopping it . . .
something she— . . . something she had to— . . . what? . . .
who? . . . no! . . . she! . . . (*pause and movement 3*) . . .
something she had to— . . . what? . . . the buzzing? . . . yes
. . . all the time the buzzing . . . dull roar . . . in the skull
. . . and the beam . . . ferreting around . . . painless . . . so
far . . . ha! . . . so far . . . then thinking . . . oh long after
. . . sudden flash . . . perhaps something she had to . . . had
to . . . tell . . . could that be it? . . . something she had to
. . . tell . . . tiny little thing . . . before its time . . . godforsaken hole . . . no love . . . spared that . . . speechless all her
days . . . practically speechless . . . how she survived! . . . that
time in court . . . what had she to say for herself . . . guilty
or not guilty . . . stand up woman . . . speak up woman . . .
stood there staring into space . . . mouth half open as usual
. . . waiting to be led away . . . glad of the hand on her arm
. . . now this . . . something she had to tell . . . could that
be it? . . . something that would tell . . . how it was . . .
how she— . . . what? . . . had been? . . . yes . . . something
that would tell how it had been . . . how she had lived . . .
lived on and on . . . guilty or not . . . on and on . . . to be sixty
. . . something she— . . . what? . . . seventy? . . . good God!
. . . on and on to be seventy . . . something she didn't
know herself . . . wouldn't know if she heard . . . then

forgiven . . . God is love . . . tender mercies . . . new every morning . . . back in the field . . . April morning . . . face in the grass . . . nothing but the larks . . . pick it up there . . . get on with it from there . . . another few— . . . what? . . . not that? . . . nothing to do with that? . . . nothing she could tell? . . . all right . . . nothing she could tell . . . try something else . . . think of something else . . . oh long after . . . sudden flash . . . not that either . . . all right . . . something else again . . . so on . . . hit on it in the end . . . think everything keep on long enough . . . then forgiven . . . back in the— . . . what? . . . not that either? . . . nothing to do with that either? . . . nothing she could think? . . . all right . . . nothing she could tell . . . nothing she could think . . . nothing she— . . . what? . . . who? . . . no! . . . she! . . . (*pause and movement 4*) . . . tiny little thing . . . out before its time . . . godforsaken hole . . . no love . . . spared that . . . speechless all her days . . . practically speechless . . . even to herself . . . never out loud . . . but not completely . . . sometimes sudden urge . . . once or twice a year . . . always winter some strange reason . . . the long evenings . . . hours of darkness . . . sudden urge to . . . tell . . . then rush out stop the first she saw . . . nearest lavatory . . . start pouring it out . . . steady stream . . . mad stuff . . . half the vowels wrong . . . no one could follow . . . till she saw the stare she was getting . . . then die of shame . . . crawl back in . . . once or twice a year . . . always winter some strange reason . . . long hours of darkness . . . now this . . . this . . . quicker and quicker . . . the words . . . the brain . . . flickering away like mad . . . quick grab and on . . . nothing there . . . on somewhere else . . . try somewhere else . . . all the time something begging . . . something in her begging . . . begging it all to stop . . . unanswered . . . prayer unanswered . . . or unheard . . . too faint . . . so on . . . keep on . . . trying . . . not knowing what . . . what she was trying . . . what to try . . . whole body like gone . . . just the mouth . . . like maddened . . . so on . . . keep— . . . what? . . . the buzzing? . . . yes . . . all the time the buzzing . . . dull roar like falls . . . in the skull . . . and the beam . . . poking around . . . painless . . . so far . . . ha! . . . so far . . . all that . . . keep on . . . not knowing what . . . what she was— . . . what? . . . who? . . . no! . . . she! . . . SHE! . . . (*pause*) . . . what she was trying . . . what to try . . . no matter . . . keep on . . . (*curtain starts down*) . . . hit on it in the end . . . then back . . . God is love . . . tender mercies . . . new every morning . . . back in the field . . . April morning . . . face in the grass . . . nothing but the larks . . . pick it up—

Curtain fully down. House dark. Voice continues behind curtain, unintelligible, 10 seconds, ceases as house lights up.

That Time

That Time

That Time was first performed at the Royal Court Theatre in the spring of 1976 during a season mounted to mark the author's seventieth birthday.

NOTE

Moments of one and the same voice A B C relay one another without solution of continuity—apart from the two 10-second breaks. Yet the switch from one to another must be clearly faintly perceptible. If threefold source and context prove insufficient to produce this effect it should be assisted mechanically (e.g. threefold pitch).

Curtain. Stage in darkness. Fade up to LISTENER's *face about ten feet above stage level midstage off centre.*

Old white face, long flaring white hair as if seen from above outspread.

Voices A B C *are his own coming to him from both sides and above. They modulate back and forth without any break in general flow except where silence indicated. See* NOTE.

Silence 7 seconds. LISTENER's *eyes are open. His breath audible, slow and regular.*

A: that time you went back that last time to look was the ruin still there where you hid as a child when was that (*eyes close*) grey day took the eleven to the end of the line and on from there no no trams then all gone long ago that time you went back to look was the ruin still there where you hid as a child that last time not a tram left in the place only the old rails when was that

C: when you went in out of the rain always winter then

always raining that time in the Portrait Gallery in off the
street out of the cold and rain slipped in when no one was
looking and through the rooms shivering and dripping till
you found a seat marble slab and sat down to rest and dry
off and on to hell out of there when was that

B: on the stone together in the sun on the stone at the edge
of the little wood and as far as eye could see the wheat
turning yellow vowing every now and then you loved each
other just a murmur not touching or anything of that
nature you one end of the stone she the other long low
stone like millstone no looks just there together on the
stone in the sun with the little wood behind gazing at the
wheat or eyes closed all still no sign of life not a soul
abroad no sound

A: straight off the ferry and up with the nightbag to the high
street neither right nor left not a curse for the old scenes
the old names straight up the rise from the wharf to the
high street and there not a wire to be seen only the old
rails all rust when was that was your mother ah for God's
sake all gone long ago that time you went back that last
time to look was the ruin still there where you hid as a
child someone's folly

C: was your mother ah for God's sake all gone long ago all
dust the lot you the last huddled up on the slab in the old
green greatcoat with your arms round you whose else
hugging you for a bit of warmth to dry off and on to hell
out of there and on to the next not a living soul in the
place only yourself and the odd attendant drowsing
around in his felt shufflers not a sound to be heard only
every now and then a shuffle of felt drawing near then
dying away

B: all still just the leaves and ears and you too still on the stone in a daze no sound not a word only every now and then to vow you loved each other just a murmur one thing could ever bring tears till they dried up altogether that thought when it came up among the others floated up that scene

A: Foley was it Foley's Folly bit of a tower still standing all the rest rubble and nettles where did you sleep no friend all the homes gone was it that kip on the front where you no she was with you then still with you then just the one night in any case off the ferry one morning and back on her the next to look was the ruin still there where none ever came where you hid as a child slip off when no one was looking and hide there all day long on a stone among the nettles with your picture-book

C: till you hoisted your head and there before your eyes when they opened a vast oil black with age and dirt someone famous in his time some famous man or woman or even child such as a young prince or princess some young prince or princess of the blood black with age behind the glass where gradually as you peered trying to make it out gradually of all things a face appeared had you swivel on the slab to see who it was was there at your elbow

B: on the stone in the sun gazing at the wheat or the sky or the eyes closed nothing to be seen but the wheat turning yellow and the blue sky vowing every now and then you loved each other just a murmur tears without fail till they dried up altogether suddenly there in whatever thoughts you might be having whatever scenes perhaps way back in childhood or the womb worst of all or that old Chinaman

That Time

long before Christ born with long white hair

C: never the same after that never quite the same but that was nothing new if it wasn't this it was that common occurrence something you could never be the same after crawling about year after year sunk in your lifelong mess muttering to yourself who else you'll never be the same after this you were never the same after that

A: or talking to yourself who else out loud imaginary conversations there was childhood for you ten or eleven on a stone among the giant nettles making it up now one voice now another till you were hoarse and they all sounded the same well on into the night some moods in the black dark or moonlight and they all out on the roads looking for you

B: or by the window in the dark harking to the owl not a thought in your head till hard to believe harder and harder to believe you ever told anyone you loved them or anyone you till just one of those things you kept making up to keep the void out just another of those old tales to keep the void from pouring in on top of you the shroud

Silence 10 seconds. Breath audible. After 3 seconds eyes open.

C: never the same but the same as what for God's sake did you ever say I to yourself in your life come on now (*eyes close*) could you ever say I to yourself in your life turning-point that was a great word with you before they dried up altogether always having turning-points and never but the one the first and last that time curled up worm in slime when they lugged you out and wiped you off and

straightened you up never another after that never looked
back after that was that the time or was that another time
B: muttering that time together on the stone in the sun or
that time together on the towpath or that time together in
the sand that time that time making it up from there as
best you could always together somewhere in the sun on
the towpath facing downstream into the sun sinking and
the bits of flotsam coming from behind and drifting on or
caught in the reeds the dead rat it looked like came on you
from behind and went drifting on till you could see it
no more
A: that time you went back to look was the ruin still there
where you hid as a child that last time straight off the
ferry and up the rise to the high street to catch the eleven
neither right nor left only one thought in your head not a
curse for the old scenes the old names just head down
press on up the rise to the top and there stood waiting
with the nightbag till the truth began to dawn
C: when you started not knowing who you were from Adam
trying how that would work for a change not knowing
who you were from Adam no notion who it was saying
what you were saying whose skull you were clapped up in
whose moan had you the way you were was that the time
or was that another time there alone with the portraits of
the dead black with dirt and antiquity and the dates on the
frames in case you might get the century wrong not
believing it could be you till they put you out in the rain
at closing-time
B: no sight of the face or any other part never turned to her
nor she to you always parallel like on an axle-tree never
turned to each other just blurs on the fringes of the field

no touching or anything of that nature always space between if only an inch no pawing in the manner of flesh and blood no better than shades no worse if it wasn't for the vows

A: no getting out to it that way so what next no question of asking not another word to the living as long as you lived so foot it up in the end to the station bowed half double get out to it that way all closed down and boarded up Doric terminus of the Great Southern and Eastern all closed down and the colonnade crumbling away so what next

C: the rain and the old rounds trying making it up that way as you went along how it would work that way for a change never having been how never having been would work the old rounds trying to wangle you into it tottering and muttering all over the parish till the words dried up and the head dried up and the legs dried up whosever they were or it gave up whoever it was

B: stock still always stock still like that time on the stone or that time in the sand stretched out parallel in the sand in the sun gazing up at the blue or eyes closed blue dark blue dark stock still side by side scene float up and there you were wherever it was

A: gave it up gave up and sat down on the steps in the pale morning sun no those steps got no sun somewhere else then gave up and off somewhere else and down on a step in the pale sun a doorstep say someone's doorstep for it to be time to get on the night ferry and out to hell out of there no need sleep anywhere not a curse for the old scenes the old names the passers pausing to gape at you quick gape then pass pass on pass by on the other side

B: stock still side by side in the sun then sink and vanish without your having stirred any more than the two knobs on a dumbbell except the lids and every now and then the lips to vow and all around too all still all sides wherever it might be no stir or sound only faintly the leaves in the little wood behind or the ears or the bent or the reeds as the case might be of man no sight of man or beast no sight or sound

C: always winter then always raining always slipping in somewhere when no one would be looking in off the street out of the cold and rain in the old green holeproof coat your father left you places you hadn't to pay to get in like the Public Library that was another great thing free culture far from home or the Post Office that was another another place another time

A: huddled on the doorstep in the old green greatcoat in the pale sun with the nightbag needless on your knees not knowing where you were little by little not knowing where you were or when you were or what for place might have been uninhabited for all you knew like that time on the stone the child on the stone where none ever came

Silence 10 seconds. Breath audible. After 3 seconds eyes open.

B: or alone in the same the same scenes making it up that way to keep it going keep it out on the stone (*eyes close*) alone on the end of the stone with the wheat and blue or the towpath alone on the towpath with the ghosts of the mules the drowned rat or bird or whatever it was floating

[34]

off into the sunset till you could see it no more nothing stirring only the water and the sun going down till it went down and you vanished all vanished

A: none ever came but the child on the stone among the giant nettles with the light coming in where the wall had crumbled away poring on his book well on into the night some moods the moonlight and they all out on the roads looking for him or making up talk breaking up two or more talking to himself being together that way where none ever came

C: always winter then endless winter year after year as if it couldn't end the old year never end like time could go no further that time in the Post Office all bustle Christmas bustle in off the street when no one was looking out of the cold and rain pushed open the door like anyone else and straight for the table neither right nor left with all the forms and the pens on their chains sat down first vacant seat and were taking a look round for a change before drowsing away

B: or that time alone on your back in the sand and no vows to break the peace when was that an earlier time a later time before she came after she went or both before she came after she was gone and you back in the old scene wherever it might be might have been the same old scene before as then then as after with the rat or the wheat the yellowing ears or that time in the sand the glider passing over that time you went back soon after long after

A: eleven or twelve in the ruin on the flat stone among the nettles in the dark or moonlight muttering away now one voice now another there was childhood for you till there on the step in the pale sun you heard yourself at it again not a curse for the passers pausing to gape at the scandal huddled there in the sun where it had no warrant clutching the nightbag drooling away out loud eyes closed and the white hair pouring out down from under the hat and so sat on in that pale sun forgetting it all

C: perhaps fear of ejection having clearly no warrant in the place to say nothing of the loathsome appearance so this look round for once at your fellow bastards thanking God for once bad and all as you were you were not as they till it dawned that for all the loathing you were getting you might as well not have been there at all the eyes passing over you and through you like so much thin air was that the time or was that another time another place another time

B: the glider passing over never any change same blue skies nothing ever changed but she with you there or not on your right hand always the right hand on the fringe of the field and every now and then in the great peace like a whisper so faint she loved you hard to believe you even you made up that bit till the time came in the end

A: making it all up on the doorstep as you went along making yourself all up again for the millionth time forgetting it all where you were and what for Foley's Folly and the lot the child's ruin you came to look was it still there to hide in again till it was night and time to go till that time came

C: the Library that was another another place another time that time you slipped in off the street out of the cold and rain when no one was looking what was it then you were never the same after never again after something to do with dust something the dust said sitting at the big round

table with a bevy of old ones poring on the·page and not
a sound

B: that time in the end when you tried and couldn't by the
window in the dark and the owl flown to hoot at someone
else or back with a shrew to its hollow tree and not
another sound hour after hour hour after hour not a sound
when you tried and tried and couldn't any more no words
left to keep it out so gave it up gave up there by the
window in the dark or moonlight gave up for good and let
it in and nothing the worse a great shroud billowing in all
over you on top of you and little or nothing the worse
little or nothing

A: back down to the wharf with the nightbag and the old
green greatcoat your father left you trailing the ground
and the white hair pouring out down from under the hat
till that time came on down neither right nor left not a
curse for the old scenes the old names not a thought in
your head only get back on board and away to hell out of
it and never come back or was that another time all that
another time was there ever any other time but that time
away to hell out of it all and never come back

C: not a sound only the old breath and the leaves turning and
then suddenly this dust whole place suddenly full of dust
when you opened your eyes from floor to ceiling nothing
only dust and not a sound only what was it it said come
and gone was that it something like that come and gone
come and gone no one come and gone in no time gone in
no time

*Silence 10 seconds. Breath audible. After 3 seconds eyes
open. After 5 seconds smile, toothless for preference. Hold 5
seconds till fade out and curtain.*

Footfalls

Footfalls

Footfalls was first performed at the Royal Court Theatre in the spring of 1976 during a season mounted to mark the author's seventieth birthday.

MAY (M), *dishevelled grey hair, worn grey wrap hiding feet, trailing.*

WOMAN's *voice* (V) *from dark upstage.*

Strip: downstage, parallel with front, length nine steps, width one metre, a little off centre audience right.

$$L \overline{\begin{array}{c} r \quad l \quad r \quad l \quad r \quad l \quad r \quad l \quad r \\ \hline l \quad r \quad l \quad r \quad l \quad r \quad l \quad r \quad l \end{array}} R$$

Pacing: starting with right foot (r) from right (R) to left (L), with left foot (l) from L to R.

Turn: rightabout at L, leftabout at R.

Steps: clearly audible rhythmic tread.

Lighting: dim, strongest at floor level, less on body, least on head.

Voices: both low and slow throughout.

Curtain. Stage in darkness. Faint single chime. Pause as echoes die. Fade up to dim on strip. Rest in darkness. M discovered pacing approaching L. Turns at L, paces three more lengths, halts facing front at R.

Pause.

M: Mother. (*Pause. No louder.*) Mother.

Pause.

V: Yes, May.

M: Were you asleep?

V: Deep asleep. (*Pause.*) I heard you in my deep sleep. (*Pause.*) There is no sleep so deep I would not hear you there. (*Pause.* M *resumes pacing. Four lengths. After first length, synchronous with steps.*) . . . . seven eight nine wheel . . . . seven eight nine wheel. (*Free.*) Will you not try to snatch a little sleep?

M *halts facing front at R. Pause.*

M: Would you like me to inject you . . . again?

V: Yes, but it is too soon.

Pause.

M: Would you like me to change your position . . . again?

V: Yes, but it is too soon.

Pause.

M: Straighten your pillows? (*Pause.*) Change your drawsheet? (*Pause.*) Pass you the bedpan? (*Pause.*) The warming-pan? (*Pause.*) Dress your sores? (*Pause.*) Sponge you down? (*Pause.*) Moisten your poor lips? (*Pause.*) Pray with you? (*Pause.*) For you? (*Pause.*) Again.

Pause.

V: Yes, but it is too soon.

Pause. M *resumes pacing, after one length halts facing front at L. Pause.*

M: What age am I now?
V: And I? (*Pause. No louder.*) And I?
M: Ninety.
V: So much?
M: Eighty-nine, ninety.
V: I had you late. (*Pause.*) In life. (*Pause.*) Forgive me . . . again. (*Pause. No louder.*) Forgive me . . . again.

Pause.

M: What age am I now?
V: In your forties.
M: So little?
V: I'm afraid so. (*Pause.* M *resumes pacing. After first turn at R.*) May. (*Pause. No louder.*) May.
M (*pacing*): Yes, Mother.
V: Will you never have done? (*Pause.*) Will you never have done . . . revolving it all?
M (*halting*): It?
V: It all. (*Pause.*) In your poor mind. (*Pause.*) It all. (*Pause.*) It all.

M *resumes pacing. Five seconds. Fade out on strip. All in darkness. Steps cease.*

Long pause.

Chime a little fainter. Pause for echoes. Fade up to a little less on strip. Rest in darkness. M discovered facing front at R.

Pause.

V: I walk here now. (*Pause.*) Rather I come and stand. (*Pause.*) At nightfall. (*Pause.*) She fancies she is alone. (*Pause.*) See how still she stands, how stark, with her face to the wall. (*Pause.*) How outwardly unmoved. (*Pause.*) She has not been out since girlhood. Not out since girlhood. (*Pause.*) Where is she, it may be asked. (*Pause.*) Why, in the old home, the same where she— (*Pause.*) The same where she began. (*Pause.*) Where it began. (*Pause.*) It all began. (*Pause.*) But this, this, when did this begin? (*Pause.*) When other girls of her age were out at ... lacrosse she was already here. (*Pause.*) At this. (*Pause.*) The floor here, now bare, once was— (M *begins pacing. Steps a little slower.*) But let us watch her move, in silence. (M *paces. Towards end of second length.*) Watch how feat she wheels. (M *turns, paces. Synchronous with steps third length.*) Seven eight nine wheel. (M *turns at L, paces one more length, halts facing front at R.*) I say the floor here, now bare, this strip of floor, once was carpeted, a deep pile. Till one night, while still little more than a child, she called her mother and said, Mother, this is not enough. The mother: Not enough? May—the child's given name—May: Not enough. The mother: What do you mean, May, not enough, what can you possibly mean, May, not enough? May: I mean, Mother, that I must hear the feet, however faint they fall. The mother: The motion alone is not enough? May: No, Mother, the motion alone is not enough, I must hear the feet, however faint they fall. (*Pause.* M *resumes pacing. With pacing.*) Does she still sleep, it may be asked? Yes, some nights she does, in snatches, bows her poor head against the wall and snatches a little sleep. (*Pause.*) Still speak? Yes, some nights she does, when she fancies none can hear. (*Pause.*) Tells how it was. (*Pause.*) Tries to tell how it was. (*Pause.*) It all. (*Pause.*) It all.

M *continues pacing. Five seconds. Fade out on strip. All in darkness. Steps cease.*

Long pause.

Chime a little fainter still. Pause for echoes. Fade up to a little less still on strip. Rest in darkness. M *discovered facing front at R.*

Pause.

M: Sequel. (M *begins pacing, after two lengths halts facing front at R.*) Sequel. A little later, when she was quite forgotten, she began to— (*Pause.*) A little later, when as though she had never been, it never been, she began to walk. (*Pause.*) At nightfall. (*Pause.*) Slip out at nightfall and into the little church by the north door, always locked at that hour, and walk, up and down, up and down, His poor arm. (*Pause.*) Some nights she would halt, as one frozen by some shudder of the mind, and stand stark still till she could move again. But many also were the nights when she paced without pause, up and down, up and down, before vanishing the way she came. (*Pause.*) No sound. (*Pause.*) None at least to be heard. (*Pause.*) The semblance. (*Pause. Resumes pacing. Steps a little slower still. After two lengths halts facing front at R.*) The semblance. Faint, though by no means invisible, in a certain light. (*Pause.*) Given the right light. (*Pause.*) Grey rather than white, a pale shade of grey. (*Pause.*) Tattered. (*Pause.*) A tangle of tatters. (*Pause.*) A faint tangle of pale grey tatters. (*Pause.*) Watch it pass—(*pause*)—watch her pass before the candelabrum how its flames, their light ... like moon through passing ... rack. (*Pause.*) Soon then after she was gone, as though never there, began to walk, up and down, up and down, that poor arm. (*Pause.*) At nightfall. (*Pause.*) That is to say, at certain seasons of the year, during Vespers. (*Pause.*) Necessarily. (*Pause. Resumes pacing. After one length halts facing front at L. Pause.*) Old Mrs. Winter, whom the reader will remember, old Mrs. Winter, one late autumn Sunday evening, on sitting down to supper with her daughter after worship, after a few half-hearted mouthfuls laid down her knife and fork and bowed her head. What is it, Mother, said the daughter, a most strange girl, though scarcely a girl any more ... (*brokenly*) ... dreadfully un—(*Pause. Normal voice.*) What is it, Mother, are you not feeling yourself? (*Pause.*) Mrs. W. did not at once reply. But finally, raising her head and fixing Amy—the daughter's given name, as the reader will remember—raising her head and fixing Amy full in the eye she said—(*pause*)—she murmured, fixing Amy full in the eye she murmured, Amy, did you observe anything ... strange at Evensong? Amy: No, Mother, I did not. Mrs. W: Perhaps it was just my fancy. Amy: Just what exactly, Mother, did you perhaps fancy it was? (*Pause.*) Just what exactly, Mother, did you perhaps fancy this ... strange thing was you observed? (*Pause.*) Mrs. W: You yourself observed nothing ... strange? Amy: No, Mother, I myself did not, to put it mildly. Mrs. W: What do you mean, Amy, to put it mildly, what can you possibly mean, Amy, to put it mildly? Amy: I mean, Mother, that to say I observed nothing ... strange is indeed to put it mildly. For I observed nothing of any kind, strange or otherwise. I saw nothing, heard nothing, of any kind. I was not there. Mrs. W: Not there? Amy: Not there. Mrs. W: But I heard you respond. (*Pause.*) I heard you say Amen. (*Pause.*) How could you have responded if you were not there? (*Pause.*) How could you possibly have said Amen if, as you claim, you were not there? (*Pause.*) The love of God, and the fellowship of the Holy Ghost, be with us all, now, and for evermore. Amen. (*Pause.*) I heard you distinctly. (*Pause. Resumes pacing. After five steps halts without facing front. Long pause. Resumes pacing, halts facing front at R. Long pause.*) Amy. (*Pause. No louder.*) Amy. (*Pause.*) Yes, Mother. (*Pause.*) Will you never have done? (*Pause.*) Will you never have done ... revolving it all? (*Pause.*) It? (*Pause.*) It all. (*Pause.*) In your poor mind. (*Pause.*) It all. (*Pause.*) It all.

Pause. Fade out on strip. All in darkness.

Pause.

Chime even a little fainter still. Pause for echoes. Fade up to even a little less still on strip. No trace of May. Hold fifteen seconds. Fade out.

Curtain.

Ghost Trio
A Television Play

Ghost Trio

Ghost Trio was first taped for television by the BBC in October, 1976, directed by D. McWhinnie. It will be taped again by the Süd-Deutscher Rundfunk in May, 1977, directed by Samuel Beckett, with Klaus Herm as F.

Female Voice (V)
Male Figure (F)

I.   Pre-action.
II. Action.
III. Re-action.

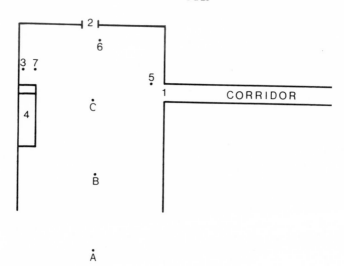

Room: 6 m. x 5 m.

1. Door.
2. Window.
3. Mirror.
4. Pallet.
5. F seated by door.
6. F at window.
7. F at head of pallet.

A   Position general view.
B   "   medium shot.
C   "   near shot of 5 and 1, 6 and 2, 7 and 3.

Ghost Trio

I

1. *Fade up to general view from A. 10″.*

2. V: Good-evening. Mine is a faint voice. Kindly tune accordingly. (*Pause.*) Good-evening. Mine is a faint voice. Kindly tune accordingly. (*Pause.*) It will not be raised, nor lowered, whatever happens. (*Pause.*) Look. (*Long pause.*) The familiar chamber. (*Pause.*) At the far end a window. (*Pause.*) On the right the indispensable door. (*Pause.*) On the left, against the wall, some kind of pallet. (*Pause.*) The light: faint, omnipresent. No visible source. As if all luminous. Faintly luminous. No shadow. (*Pause.*) No shadow. Colour: none. All grey. Shades of grey. (*Pause.*) The colour grey if you wish, shades of the colour grey. (*Pause.*) Forgive my stating the obvious. (*Pause.*) Keep that sound down. (*Pause.*) Now look closer. (*Pause.*) Floor.

3. *Cut to close-up of floor. Smooth grey rectangle 0.70 m. x 1.50 m. 5″.*

4. V: Dust. (*Pause.*) Having seen that specimen of floor you have seen it all. Wall.

5. *Cut to close-up of wall. Smooth grey rectangle 0.70 m. x 1.50 m. 5″.*

6. V: Dust.

7. *Move to second close-up of wall. Identical. 5″.*

8. V: Knowing this, the kind of floor, the kind of wall, look again.

9. *Cut to general view from A. 5".*

10. V: Door.

11. *Cut to close-up of whole door. Smooth grey rectangle 0.70 m. x 2 m. Imperceptibly ajar. No knob. Faint music. 5".*

12. V: Window.

13. *Cut to close-up of whole window. Plain sheet of glass 0.70 m. x 1.50 m. Imperceptibly ajar. No knob. 5".*

14. V: Pallet.

15. *Cut to close-up from above of whole pallet. 0.70 m. x 2 m. Grey sheet. Grey rectangular pillow at window end. 5".*

16. V: Knowing all this, the kind of pallet—

17. *Close-up of whole pallet continued. 5".*

18. V: The kind of window—

19. *Cut to close-up of whole window. 5".*

20. V: The kind of door—

21. *Cut to close-up of whole door. Faint music. 5".*

22. V: The kind of wall—

23. *Cut to close-up of wall as before. 5".*

24. V: The kind of floor.

25. *Cut to close-up of floor as before. 5".*

26. V: Look again.

27. *Cut to general view. 5".*

28. V: Sole sign of life a seated figure.

30. *Move in slowly from A to B whence medium shot of F and door. F is seated on a stool, bowed forward, face hidden, clutching with both hands a small cassette not identifiable as such at this range. Faint music. 5".*

31. *Move in from B to C whence near shot of F and door. Cassette now identifiable. Music slightly louder. 5".*

32. *Move in from C to close-up of head, hands, cassette. Clutching hands, head bowed, face hidden. Music slightly louder. 5".*

33. *Move slowly back to A via C and B (no stops). Music progressively fainter till at level of B it ceases to be heard.*

34. *General view from A. 5".*

Ends and Odds

II

All from A except 25-28.

1. V: He will now think he hears her.

2. F *raises head sharply, turns still crouched to door, fleeting face, tense pose. 5".*

3. V: No one.

4. F relapses into opening pose, bowed over cassette.

5. V: Again.

6. *Same as 2.*

7. V: Now to the door.

8. F *gets up, lays cassette on stool, goes to door, listens with right ear against door, back to camera. 5".*

9. V: No one.

10. *With right hand* F *pushes door open halfway clockwise, looks out, back to camera. 5".*

11. V: No one.

12. F *removes hand from door which closes slowly of itself, stands irresolute, back to camera. 5".*

[58]

13. V: Now to window.

14. F *goes to window, stands irresolute, back to camera. 5".*

15. *With right hand* F *pushes window open halfway clockwise, looks out, back to camera. 5".*

16. V: No one.

17. F *removes hand from window which closes slowly of itself, stands irresolute, back to camera. 5".*

18. V: Now to pallet.

19. F *goes to head of pallet (window end), stands looking down at it. 5".*

20. F *turns to wall at head of pallet, goes to wall, looks at his face in mirror hanging on wall, invisible from A.*

21. V (*surprised*): Ah!

22. *After 5"* F *bows his head, stands before mirror with bowed head. 5".*

23. V: Now to door.

24. F *goes to stool, takes up cassette, sits, settles into opening pose, bowed over cassette. 5".*

25. *Same as I.30.*

26. *Same as I.31.*

27. *Same as I.32.*

28. *Same as I.33.*

29. *Same as I.34.*

30. v: He will now again think he hears her.

31. *Same as II.2.*

32. F *gets up, goes to door, opens it as before, looks out, stoops forward. 10".*

33. F *straightens up, releases door which closes slowly of itself, stands irresolute, goes to stool, takes up cassette, sits irresolute, settles finally into opening pose, bowed over cassette. 5".*

34. *Faint music audible for first time at A. It grows louder. 5".*

35. v: Stop.

36. *Music stops. General view from A. 5".*

37. v: Repeat.

Ghost Trio

III

1. *Immediately after "Repeat" cut to near shot from C of* F *and door. Music audible. 5".*

2. *Move in to close-up of head, hands, cassette. Music slightly louder. 5".*

3. *Music stops. Action II.2. 5".*

4. *Action II.4. Music resumes. 5".*

5. *Move back to near shot from C of* F *and door. Music audible. 5".*

6. *Music stops. Action II.2. Near shot from C of* F *and door. 5".*

7. *Action II.8. Sound of cassette laid on stool. Near shot from C of stool, cassette,* F *with right ear to door. 5".*

8. *Action II.10. Crescendo creak of door opening. Near shot from C of stool, cassette,* F *with right hand holding door open. 5".*

9. *Cut to view of corridor seen from door. Long narrow (0.70 m.) grey rectangle between grey walls, empty, far end in darkness. 5".*

10. *Cut back to near shot from C of stool, cassette,* F *holding door open. 5".*

11. *Action II.12. Decrescendo creak of door slowly closing. Near shot from C of stool, cassette,* F *standing irresolute, door. 5".*

12. *Cut to close-up from above of cassette on stool, small grey rectangle on larger rectangle of seat. 5".*

13. *Cut back to near shot of stool, cassette,* F *standing irresolute, door. 5".*

14. *Action II.14 seen from C. Near shot from C of* F *and window. 5".*

15. *Action II.15 seen from C. Crescendo creak of window opening. Faint sound of rain. Near shot from C of* F *with right hand holding window open. 5".*

16. *Cut to view from window. Night. Rain falling in dim light. Sound of rain slightly louder. 5".*

17. *Cut back to near shot from C of* F *with right hand holding window open. Faint sound of rain. 5".*

18. *Action II.17 seen from C. Decrescendo creak of window slowly closing. Near shot from C of* F *and window. 5".*

19. *Action II.19 seen from C. Near shot from C of* F *mirror, head of pallet.*

20. *Cut to close-up from above of whole pallet.*

21. *Move down to tighter close-up of pallet moving slowly from pillow to foot and back to pillow. 5" on pillow.*

22. *Move back to close-up from above of whole pallet. 5".*

23. *Cut back to near shot from C of F, mirror, head of pallet. 5".*

24. *Cut to close-up of mirror reflecting nothing. Small grey rectangle (same dimensions as cassette) against larger rectangle of wall. 5".*

25. *Cut back to near shot from C of F, head of pallet. 5".*

26. *Action II.20 seen from C. Near shot from C of F and mirror. 5".*

27. *Cut to close-up of F's face in mirror. 5". Eyes close. 5". Eyes open. 5". Head bows. Top of head in mirror. 5".*

28. *Cut back to near shot from C of F with bowed head, mirror, head of pallet. 5".*

29. *Action II.24 seen from C. Near shot from C of F settling into opening pose. Music audible once settled. 10".*

30. *Music stops. Action II.2 seen from C. Faint sound of steps approaching. They stop. Faint sound of knock on door. 5". Second knock, no louder. 5".*

31. *Action II.32 seen from C. Crescendo creak of door*

opening. Near shot from C of stool, cassette, F *holding door open, stooping forward. 10".*

32. *Cut to near shot of small boy full length in corridor before open door. Dressed in black oilskin with hood glistening with rain. White face raised to invisible* F. *5". Boy shakes head faintly. Face still, raised. 5". Boy shakes head again. Face still, raised. 5". Boy turns and goes. Sound of receding steps. Register from same position his slow recession till he vanishes in dark at end of corridor. 5" on empty corridor.*

33. *Cut back to near shot from C of stool, cassette,* F *holding door open. 5".*

34. *Action II.33 seen from C. Decrescendo creak of door slowly closing. 5".*

35. *Cut to general view from A. 5".*

36. *Music audible at A. It grows. 10".*

37. *With growing music move in slowly to close-up of head bowed right down over cassette now held in arms and invisible. Hold till end of Largo.*

38. *Silence.* F *raises head. Face seen clearly for second time. 10".*

39. *Move slowly back to A.*

40. *General view from A. 5″.*

41. *Fade out.*

MUSIC

From Largo of Beethoven's 5th Piano Trio ("The Ghost").

I.11	Beginning bar 47
I.21	″ ″ 49
I.30-33	″ ″ 19
II.25-28	″ ″ 64
II.34-35	″ ″ 70
III.1-2 4-5	″ ″ 26
III.29	″ ″ 68
III.36 to end	″ ″ 70

Odds
Roughs for Theatre and Radio

Theatre I

Theatre I

Street corner. Ruins. A, *blind, sitting on a folding stool, scrapes his fiddle. Beside him the case, half open, upended, surmounted by alms bowl. He stops playing, turns his head audience right, listens.*

Pause.

A: A penny for a poor old man, a penny for a poor old man. (*Silence. He resumes playing, stops again, turns his head right, listens. Enter* B, *right, in a wheelchair which he propels by means of a pole. He halts. Irritated.*) A penny for a poor old man!

Pause.

B: Music! (*Pause.*) So it is not a dream. At last! Nor a vision, they are mute and I am mute before them (*He advances, halts, looks into bowl. Without emotion.*) Poor wretch.

(*Pause.*) Now I may go back, the mystery is over. (*He pushes himself backwards, halts.*) Unless we join together, and live together, till death ensue. (*Pause.*) What would you say to that, Billy, may I call you Billy, like my son? (*Pause.*) Do you like company, Billy? (*Pause.*) Do you like tinned food, Billy?

A: What tinned food?

B: Corned beef, Billy, just corned beef. Enough to keep body and soul together, till summer, with care. (*Pause.*) No? (*Pause.*) A few potatoes too, a few pounds of potatoes too. (*Pause.*) Do you like potatoes, Billy? (*Pause.*) We might even let them sprout and then, when the time came, put them in the ground, we might even try that. (*Pause.*) I would choose the place and you would put them in the ground. (*Pause.*) No?

Pause.

A: How are the trees doing?
B: Hard to say. It's winter, you know.

Pause.

A: Is it day or night?
B: Oh . . . (*he looks at the sky*) . . . day, if you like. No sun of course, otherwise you wouldn't have asked. (*Pause.*) Do you follow my reasoning? (*Pause.*) Have you your wits about you, Billy, have you still some of your wits about you?
A: But light?
B: Yes. (*Looks at sky.*) Yes, light, there is no other word for it. (*Pause.*) Shall I describe it to you? (*Pause.*) Shall I try to give you an idea of this light?
A: It seems to me sometimes I spend the night here, playing and listening. I used to feel twilight gather and make myself ready. I put away fiddle and bowl and had only to get to my feet, when she took me by the hand.

Pause.

B: She?
A: My woman. (*Pause.*) A woman. (*Pause.*) But now . . .

Theatre I

Pause.

B: Now?

A: When I set out I don't know, and when I get here I don't know, and while I am here I don't know, whether it is day or night.

B: You were not always as you are. What befell you? Women? Gambling? God?

A: I was always as I am.

B: Come!

A (*violently*): I was always as I am, crouched in the dark, scratching an old jangle to the four winds!

B (*violently*): We had our women, hadn't we? You yours to lead you by the hand and I mine to get me out of the chair in the evening and back into it again in the morning and to push me as far as the corner when I went out of my mind.

A: Cripple? (*Without emotion.*) Poor wretch.

B: Only one problem: the about-turn. I often felt, as I struggled, that it would be quicker to go on, right round the world. Till the day I realized I could go home backwards. (*Pause.*) For example, I am at A. (*He pushes himself forward a little, halts.*) I push on to B. (*He pushes himself back a little, halts.*) And I return to A. (*With élan.*) The straight line! The vacant space! (*Pause.*) Do I begin to move you?

A: Sometimes I hear steps. Voices. I say to myself, They are coming back, some are coming back, to try and settle again, or to look for something they had left behind, or to look for someone they had left behind.

B: Come back! (*Pause.*) Who would want to come back here? (*Pause.*) And you never called out? (*Pause.*) Cried out?

[73]

(*Pause.*) No?

A: Have you observed nothing?

B: Oh me you know, observe . . . I sit there, in my lair, in my chair, in the dark, twenty-three hours out of the twenty-four. (*Violently.*) What would you have me observe? (*Pause.*) Do you think we would make a match, now you are getting to know me?

A: Corned beef, did you say?

B: Apropos, what have you been living on, all this time? You must be famished.

A: There are things lying around.

B: Edible?

A: Sometimes.

B: Why don't you let yourself die?

A: On the whole I have been lucky. The other day I tripped over a sack of nuts.

B: No!

A: A little sack, full of nuts, in the middle of the road.

B: Yes, all right, but why don't you let yourself die?

A: I have thought of it.

B (*irritated*): But you don't do it!

A: I'm not unhappy enough. (*Pause.*) That was always my unhap, unhappy, but not unhappy enough.

B: But you must be every day a little more so.

A (*violently*): I am not unhappy enough!

Pause.

B: If you ask me we were made for each other.

A (*comprehensive gesture*): What does it all look like now?

B: Oh me you know . . . I never go far, just a little up and

[74]

down before my door. I never yet pushed on to here till now.

A: But you look about you?

B: No no.

A: After all those hours of darkness you don't—

B (*violently*): No! (*Pause.*) Of course if you wish me to look about me I shall. And if you care to push me about I shall try to describe the scene, as we go along.

A: You mean you would guide me? I wouldn't get lost any more?

B: Exactly. I would say, Easy, Billy, we're heading for a great muckheap, turn back and wheel left when I give you the word.

A: You'd do that!

B (*pressing his advantage*): Easy, Billy, easy, I see a round tin over there in the gutter, perhaps it's soup, or baked beans.

A: Baked beans!

Pause.

B: Are you beginning to like me? (*Pause.*) Or is it only my imagination?

A: Baked beans! (*He gets up, puts down fiddle and bowl on the stool and gropes towards* B.) Where are you?

B: Here, dear fellow. (A *lays hold of the chair and starts pushing it blindly.*) Stop!

A (*pushing the chair*): It's a gift! A gift!

B: Stop! (*He strikes behind him with the pole.* A *lets go the chair, recoils. Pause.* A *gropes towards his stool, halts, lost.*) Forgive me! (*Pause.*) Forgive me, Billy!

A: Where am I? (*Pause.*) Where was I?

B: Now I've lost him. He was beginning to like me and I struck him. He'll leave me and I'll never see him again. I'll never see anyone again. We'll never hear the human voice again.

A: Have you not heard it enough? The same old moans and groans from the cradle to the grave.

B (*groaning*): Do something for me, before you go!

A: There! Do you hear it? (*Pause. Groaning.*) I can't go! (*Pause.*) Do you hear it?

B: You can't go?

A: I can't go without my things.

B: What good are they to you?

A: None.

B: And you can't go without them?

A: No. (*He starts groping again, halts.*) I'll find them in the end. (*Pause.*) Or leave them forever behind me.

He starts groping again.

B: Straighten my rug, I feel the cold air on my foot. (*A halts.*) I'd do it myself, but it would take too long. (*Pause.*) Do that for me, Billy. Then I may go back, settle in the old nook again and say, I have seen man for the last time, I struck him and he succoured me. (*Pause.*) Find a few rags of love in my heart and die reconciled, with my species. (*Pause.*) What has you gaping at me like that? (*Pause.*) Have I said something I shouldn't have? (*Pause.*) What does my soul look like?

A *gropes towards him.*

[76]

Theatre I

A: Make a sound.

B *makes one.* A *gropes towards it, halts.*

B: Have you no sense of smell either?

A: It's the same smell everywhere. (*He stretches out his hand.*) Am I within reach of your hand?

He stands motionless with outstretched hand.

B: Wait, you're not going to do me a service for nothing? (*Pause.*) I mean unconditionally? (*Pause.*) Good God!

Pause. He takes A'*s hand and draws him towards him.*

A: Your foot.

B: What?

A: You said your foot.

B: Had I but known! (*Pause.*) Yes, my foot, tuck it in. (A *stoops, groping.*) On your knees, on your knees, you'll be more at your ease. (*He helps him to kneel at the right place.*) There.

A (*irritated*): Let go my hand! You want me to help you and you hold my hand! (B *lets go his hand.* A *fumbles in the rug.*) Have you only one leg?

B: Just the one.

A: And the other?

B: It went bad and was removed.

A *tucks in the foot.*

A: Will that do?

B: A little tighter. (A *tucks in tighter.*) What hands you have!

Pause.

A (*groping towards* B'*s torso*): Is all the rest there?

B: You may stand up now and ask me a favour.

A: Is all the rest there?

B: Nothing else has been removed, if that is what you mean.

A's *hand, groping higher, reaches the face, stays.*

A: Is that your face.

B: I confess it is. (*Pause.*) What else could it be? (A's *fingers stray, stay.*) That? My wen.

A: Red?

B: Purple. (A *withdraws his hand, remains kneeling.*) What hands you have!

Pause.

A: Is it still day?

B: Day? (*Looks at sky.*) If you like. (*Looks.*) There is no other word for it.

A: Will it not soon be evening?

B *stoops to* A, *shakes him.*

B: Come, Billy, get up, you're beginning to incommode me.

A: Will it not soon be night?

[78]

Theatre I

B *looks at sky.*

B: Day ... night ... (*Looks.*) It seems to me sometimes the earth must have got stuck, one sunless day, in the heart of winter, in the grey of evening. (*Stoops to* A, *shakes him.*) Come on, Billy, up, you're beginning to embarrass me.

A: Is there grass anywhere?

B: I see none.

A (*vehement*): Is there no green anywhere?

B: There's a little moss. (*Pause.* A *clasps his hands on the rug and rests his head on them.*) Good God! Don't tell me you're going to pray?

A: No.

B: Or weep?

A: No. (*Pause.*) I could stay like that for ever, with my head on an old man's knees.

B: Knee. (*Shaking him roughly.*) Get up, can't you!

A (*settling himself more comfortably*): What peace! (B *pushes him roughly away,* A *falls to his hands and knees.*) Dora used to say, the days I hadn't earned enough, You and your harp! You'd do better crawling on all fours, with your father's medals pinned to your arse and a money box round your neck. You and your harp! Who do you think you are? And she made me sleep on the floor. (*Pause.*) Who I thought I was ... (*Pause.*) Ah that ... I never could ... (*Pause. He gets up.*) Never could ... (*He starts groping again for his stool, halts, listens.*) If I listened long enough I'd hear it, a string would give.

B: Your harp? (*Pause.*) What's all this about a harp?

A: I once had a little harp. Be still and let me listen.

[79]

Pause.

B: How long are you going to stay like that?
A: I can stay for hours listening to all the sounds.

They listen.

B: What sounds?
A: I don't know what they are.

They listen.

B: I can see it. (*Pause.*) I can—
A (*imploring*): Will you not be still?
B: No! (A *takes his head in his hands.*) I can see it clearly, over there on the stool. (*Pause.*) What if I took it, Billy, and made off with it? (*Pause.*) Eh Billy, what would you say to that? (*Pause.*) There might be another old man, some day, would come out of his hole and find you playing the mouth-organ. And you'd tell him of the little fiddle you once had. (*Pause.*) Eh Billy? (*Pause.*) Or singing. (*Pause.*) Eh Billy, what would you say to that? (*Pause.*) There croaking to the winter wind (*rime with unkind*), having lost his little mouth-organ. (*He pokes him in the back with the pole.*) Eh Billy?

A *whirls round, seizes the end of the pole and wrenches it from* B's grasp.

(*Translated by the author.*)

[80]

Theatre II

Theatre II

Upstage centre high double window open on bright night-sky. Moon invisible.

Downstage audience left, equidistant from wall and axis of window, small table and chair. On table an extinguished reading-lamp and a briefcase crammed with documents.

Downstage right, forming symmetry, identical table and chair. Extinguished lamp only.

Downstage left door.

Standing motionless before left half of window with his back to stage, C.

Long pause.

Enter A. *He closes door, goes to table on right and sits with his back to right wall. Pause. He switches on lamp, takes out his watch, consults it and lays it on the table. Pause. He switches off.*

Long pause.

Enter B. *He closes door, goes to table on left and sits with his back to left wall. Pause. He switches on lamp, opens briefcase and empties contents on table. He looks round, sees* A.

B: Well!
A: Hsst Switch off. (B *switches off. Long pause. Low.*) What

[83]

a night! (*Long pause. Musing.*) I still don't understand. (*Pause.*) Why he needs our services. (*Pause.*) A man like him. (*Pause.*) And why we give them free. (*Pause.*) Men like us. (*Pause.*) Mystery. (*Pause.*) Ah well . . . (*Pause. He switches on.*) Shall we go? (B *switches on, rummages in his papers.*) The crux. (B *rummages.*) We sum up and clear out. (B *rummages.*) Set to go?

B: Rearing.

A: We attend.

B: Let him jump.

A: When?

B: Now.

A: From where?

B: From here will do. Three to three and a half metres per floor, say twenty-five in all.

Pause.

A: I could have sworn we were only on the sixth. (*Pause.*) He runs no risk?

B: He has only to land on his arse, the way he lived. The spine snaps and the tripes explode.

Pause. A *gets up, goes to the window, leans out, looks down. He straightens up, looks at the sky. Pause. He goes back to his seat.*

A: Full moon.

B: Not quite. Tomorrow.

A *takes a little diary from his pocket.*

[84]

Theatre II

A: What's the date?

B: Twenty-fourth. Twenty-fifth tomorrow.

A (*turning pages*): Nineteen . . . twenty-two . . . twenty-four. (*Reads.*) "Our Lady of Succour. Full moon." (*He puts back the diary in his pocket.*) We were saying then . . . what was it . . . let him jump. Our conclusion. Right?

B: Work, family, third fatherland, cunt, finances, art and nature, heart and conscience, health, housing conditions, God and man, so many disasters.

Pause.

A (*meditative*): Does it follow? (*Pause.*) Does it follow? (*Pause.*) And his sense of humour? Of proportion?

B: Swamped.

Pause.

A: May we not be mistaken?

B (*indignant*): We have been to the best sources. All weighed and weighed again, checked and verified. Not a word here (*brandishing sheaf of papers*) that is not cast iron. Tied together like a cathedral. (*He flings down the papers on the table. They scatter on the floor.*) Shit!

He picks them up. A *raises his lamp and shines it about him.*

A: Seen worse dumps. (*Turning towards window.*) Worse outlooks. (*Pause.*) Is that Jupiter we see?

[85]

Pause.

B: Where?

A: Switch off. (*They switch off.*) It must be.

B (*irritated*): Where?

A (*irritated*): There. (B *cranes.*) There, on the right, in the corner.

Pause.

B: No. It twinkles.

A: What is it then?

B (*indifferent*): No idea. Sirius. (*He switches on.*) Well? Do we work or play? (A *switches on.*) You forget this is not his home. He's only here to take care of the cat. At the end of the month shoosh back to the barge. (*Pause. Louder.*) You forget this is not his home.

A (*irritated*): I forget, I forget! And he, does he not forget? (*With passion.*) But that's what saves us!

B (*searching through his papers*): Memory . . . memory . . . (*He takes up a sheet.*) I quote: "An elephant's for the eating cares, a sparrow's for the Lydian airs." Testimony of Mr. Swell, organist at Seaton Sluice and lifelong friend.

Pause.

A (*glum*): Tsstss!

B: I quote: "Questioned on this occasion"—open brackets— "(judicial separation)"—close brackets—"regarding the deterioration of our relations, all he could adduce was the five or six miscarriages which clouded"—open brackets—

"(oh through no act of mine!)"—close brackets—"the early days of our union and the veto which in consequence I had finally to oppose"—open brackets—"(oh not for want of inclination!)"—close brackets—"to anything remotely resembling the work of love. But on the subject of our happiness"—open brackets—"(for it too came our way, unavoidably, and here my mind goes back to the first vows exchanged at Wooton Bassett under the bastard acacias, or again to the first fifteen minutes of our wedding night at Littlestone-on-Sea, or yet again to those first long studious evenings in our nest on Commercial Road East)"—close brackets—"on the subject of our happiness not a word, Sir, not one word." Testimony of Mrs. Aspasia Budd-Croker, button designer in residence, Commercial Road East.

A (*glum*): Tsstss!

B: I quote again: "Of our national epos he remembered only the calamities, which did not prevent him from winning a minor scholarship in the subject." Testimony of Mr. Peaberry, market-gardener in the Deeping Fens and life-long friend. (*Pause.*) "Not a tear was known to fall in our family, and God knows they did in torrents, that was not caught up and piously preserved in that inexhaustible reservoir of sorrow, with the date, the hour and the occasion, and not a joy, fortunately they were few, that was not on the contrary irrevocably dissolved, as by a corrosive. In that he took after me." Testimony of the late Mrs. Darcy-Croker, woman of letters. (*Pause.*) Care for more?

A: Enough.

B: I quote: "To hear him talk about his life, after a glass or two, you would have thought he had never set foot outside hell. He had us in stitches. I worked it up into a skit that went down well." Testimony of Mr. Moore, light comedian, c/o Widow Merryweather-Moore, All Saints on the Wash, and lifelong friend.

Pause.

A (*stricken*): Tsstss! (*Pause.*) Tsstsstss!
B: You see. (*Emphatic.*) This is not his home and he knows it full well.

Pause.

A: Now let's have the positive elements.
B: Positive? You mean of a nature to make him think . . . (*hesitates, then with sudden violence*) . . . that some day things might change? Is that what you want? (*Pause. Calmer.*) There are none.
A (*wearily*): Oh yes there are, that's the beauty of it.

Pause. B *rummages in his papers.*

B (*looking up*): Forgive me, Bertrand. (*Pause. Rummages. Looks up.*) I don't know what came over me. (*Pause. Rummages. Looks up.*) A moment of consternation. (*Pause. Rummages.*) There is that incident of the lottery . . . possibly. Remember?
A: No.
B (*reading*): "Two hundred lots . . . winner receives high class watch . . . solid gold, hallmark nineteen carats, marvel

of accuracy, showing year, month, date, day, hour, minute and second, super chic, unbreakable hair spring, chrono escapement nineteen rubies, anti-shock, anti-magnetic, airtight, waterproof, stainless, self-winding, centre seconds hand, Swiss parts, de luxe lizard band."

A: What did I tell you? However unhopefully. The mere fact of chancing his luck. I knew he had a spark left in him.

B: The trouble is he didn't procure it himself. It was a gift. That you forget.

A (*irritated*): I forget, I forget! And he, does he not—. (*Pause.*) At least he kept it.

B: If you can call it that.

A: At least he accepted it. (*Pause.*) At least he didn't refuse it.

B: I quote: "The last time I laid eyes on him I was on my way to the Post Office to cash an order for back-pay. The area before the building is shut off by a row of bollards with chains hung between them. He was seated on one of these with his back to the Thompson works. To all appearances down and out. He sat doubled in two, his hands on his knees, his legs astraddle, his head sunk. For a moment I wondered if he was not vomiting. But on drawing nearer I could see he was merely scrutinizing, between his feet, a lump of dogshit. I moved it slightly with the tip of my umbrella and observed how his gaze followed the movement and fastened on the object in its new position. This at three o'clock in the afternoon if you please! I confess I had not the heart to bid him the time of day, I was overcome. I simply slipped into his hip pocket a lottery ticket I had no use for, while silently wishing him the best of luck. When two hours later I emerged from the Post Office, having cashed my order, he was at the same place and in the same attitude. I sometimes wonder if he is still alive." Testimony of Mr. Feckman, certified accountant and friend for better and for worse.

Pause.

A: Dated when?
B: Recent.
A: It has such a bygone ring. (*Pause.*) Nothing else?
B: Oh . . . bits and scraps . . . good graces of an heirless aunt . . . unfinished—
A: Hairless aunt?
B: . . . heirless aunt . . . unfinished game of chess with a correspondent in Tasmania . . . hope not dead of living to see the extermination of the species . . . literary aspirations incompletely stifled . . . bottom of a dairy-woman in Waterloo Lane . . . you see the kind of thing.

Pause.

A: We pack up this evening, right?
B: Without fail. Tomorrow we're at Bury St. Edmunds.
A (*sadly*): We'll leave him none the wiser. We'll leave him now, never to meet again, having added nothing to what he knew already.
B: All these testimonies were new to him. They will have finished him off.
A: Not necessarily. (*Pause.*) Any light on that? (*Papers.*) This is vital. (*Papers.*) Something . . . I seem to remember . . . something . . . he said himself.

B (*papers*): Under "Confidences" then. (*Brief laugh.*) Slim file. (*Papers.*) Confidences . . . confidences . . . ah!

A (*impatient*): Well?

B (*reading*): ". . . sick headaches . . . eye trouble . . . irrational fear of vipers . . . ear trouble . . ."–nothing for us there–". . .fibroid tumours . . . pathological horror of songbirds . . . throat trouble . . . need of affection . . ." –we're coming to it–". . . inner void . . . congenital timidity . . . nose trouble . . ."– ah! listen to this!– ". . . morbidly sensitive to the opinion of others . . ." (*Looks up.*) What did I tell you?

A (*glum*): Tsstss!

B: I'll read the whole passage: ". . . morbidly sensitive to the opinion of others–" (*His lamp goes out.*) Well! The bulb has blown! (*The lamp goes on again.*) No, it hasn't! Must be a faulty connection. (*Examines lamp, straightens flex.*) The flex was twisted, now all is well. (*Reading.*) ". . . morbidly sensitive–" (*The lamp goes out.*) Bugger and shit!

A: Try giving her a shake. (B *shakes the lamp. It goes on again.*) See! I picked up that wrinkle in the Band of Hope.

Pause.

B
A (*together*): ". . . morbidly sensitive–"
 Keep your hands off the table.

B: What?

A: Keep your hands off the table. If it's a connection the least jog can do it.

B (*having pulled back his chair a little way*): ". . . morbidly sensitive–"

[91]

The lamp goes out. B *bangs on the table with his fist. The lamp goes on again. Pause.*

A: Mysterious affair, electricity.

B (*hurriedly*): ". . . morbidly sensitive to the opinion of others at the time, I mean as often and for as long as they entered my awareness—" What kind of Chinese is that?

A (*nervously*): Keep going, keep going!

B: ". . . for as long as they entered my awareness, and that in either case, I mean whether such on the one hand as to give me pleasure or on the contrary on the other to cause me pain, and truth to tell—" Shit! Where's the verb?

A: What verb?

B: The main!

A: I give up.

B: Hold on till I find the verb and to hell with all this drivel in the middle. (*Reading.*) ". . . were I but . . . could I but . . ."– Jesus!–". . . though it be . . . be it but . . ."–Christ!–ah! I have it–". . . I was unfortunately incapable . . ." Done it!

A: How does it run now?

B (*solemnly*): ". . . morbidly sensitive to the opinion of others at the time . . ."–drivel drivel drivel–". . . I was unfortunately incapable—"

The lamp goes out. Long pause.

A: Would you care to change seats? (*Pause.*) You see what I mean? (*Pause.*) That you come over here with your papers and I go over there. (*Pause.*) Don't whinge, Morvan, that will get us nowhere.

B: It's my nerves. (*Pause.*) Ah if I were only twenty years younger I'd put an end to my sufferings!

A: Fie! Never say such horrid things! Even to a well-wisher!

B: May I come to you? (*Pause.*) I need animal warmth.

Pause.

A (*coldly*): As you like. (B *gets up and goes towards* A.) With your files if you don't mind. (B *goes back for papers and briefcase, returns towards* A, *puts them on* A's *table, remains standing. Pause.*) Do you want me to take you on my knees?

Pause. B *goes back for his chair, returns towards* A, *stops before* A's *table with the chair in his arms. Pause.*

B (*shyly*): May I sit beside you? (*They look at each other.*) No? (*Pause.*) Then opposite. (*He sits down opposite* A, *looks at him. Pause.*) Do we continue?

A (*forcibly*): Let's get it over and go to bed.

B *rummages in his papers.*

B: I'll take the lamp. (*He draws it towards him.*) Please God it holds out. What would we do in the dark the pair of us? (*Pause.*) Have you matches?

A: Never without. (*Pause.*) What we would do? Go and stand by the window in the starlight. (B's *lamp goes on again.*) That is to say you would.

B (*fervently*): Oh no not alone I wouldn't!

A: Pass me a sheet. (B *passes him a sheet.*) Switch off. (B

[93]

switches off.) Oh lord, yours is on again.
B: This gag has gone on long enough for me.
A: Just so. Go and switch it off.

B *goes to his table, switches off his lamp. Pause.*

B: What am I to do now? Switch it on again?
A: Come back.
B: Switch on then till I see where I'm going.

A *switches on.* B *goes back and sits down opposite* A. A *switches off, goes to window with sheet, halts, contemplates the sky.*

A: And to think all that is nuclear combustion! All that faerie! (*He stoops over sheet and reads haltingly.*) "Aged ten, runs away from home first time, brought back next day, admonished, forgiven." (*Pause.*) "Aged fifteen, runs away from home second time, dragged back a week later, thrashed, forgiven." (*Pause.*) "Aged seventeen, runs away from home third time, slinks back six months later with his tail between his legs, locked up, forgiven." (*Pause.*) "Aged seventeen, runs away from home last time, crawls back a year later on his hands and knees, kicked out, forgiven."

Pause. He moves up against window to inspect C's *face, to do which he has to lean out a little way, with his back to the void.*

B: Careful!

Theatre II

Long pause, all three dead still.

A (*sadly*): Tsstss! (*He resumes his equilibrium.*) Switch on. (B *switches on.* A *goes back to his table, sits, returns the sheet to* B.) It's heavy going, but we're nearly home.

B: How does he look.

A: Not at his best.

B: Has he still got that little smile on his face?

A: Probably.

B: What do you mean, probably, haven't you just been looking at him?

A: He didn't have it then.

B (*with satisfaction*): Ah! (*Pause.*) Could never make out what he thought he was doing with that smile on his face. And his eyes? Still goggling?

A: Shut.

B: Shut!

A: Oh it was only so as not to see me. He must have opened them again since. (*Pause. Violently.*) You'd need to stare them in the face day and night! Never take your eyes off them for a week on end! Unbeknownst to them!

Pause.

B: Looks to me we have him.

A (*impatiently*): Come on, we're getting nowhere, get on with it.

B *rummages in his papers, finds the sheet.*

[95]

B (*reading at top speed*): ". . . morbidly sensitive to the opinion of others at the time . . ."—drivel drivel drivel— ". . . I was unfortunately incapable of retaining it for more than ten or fifteen minutes at the most, that is to say the time required to take it in. From then on it might as well never have been uttered." (*Pause.*) Tsstss!

A (*with satisfaction*): You see. (*Pause.*) Where does that come in?

B: In a letter presumably never posted to an anonymous admiratrix.

A: An admiratrix? He had admiratrixes?

B: It begins: "Dear friend and admiratrix . . ." That's all we know.

A: Come, Morvan, calm yourself, letters to admiratrixes, we all know what they're worth. No need to take everything literally.

B (*violently, slapping down his hand on the pile of papers*): There's the record, closed and final. That's what we're going on. Too late now to start saying that (*slapping to his left*) is right and that (*slapping to his right*) wrong. You're a pain in the arse.

Pause.

A: Good. Let us sum up.

B: We do nothing else.

A: A black future, an unpardonable past—so far as he can remember, inducements to linger on all equally preposterous and the best advice dead letter. Agreed?

B: An heirless aunt preposterous?

A (*warmly*): He's not the interested type. (*Sternly.*) One has to consider the client's temperament. To accumulate documents is not enough.

B (*vexed, slapping on his papers*): Here, as far as I'm concerned the client is here and nowhere else.

A: All right. Is there a single reference there to personal gain? That old aunt, was he ever as much as commonly civil to her? And that dairy-woman, come to that, in all the years he's been going to her for his bit of cheddar, was he ever once wanting in respect? (*Pause.*) No, Morvan, look you—.

Feeble miaow. Pause. Second miaow, louder.

B: That must be the cat.

A: Sounds like it. (*Long pause.*) So, agreed? Black future, unpardonable—

B: As you wish. (*He starts to tidy back the papers in the briefcase. Wearily.*) Let him jump.

A: No further exhibit?

B: Let him jump, let him jump. (*He finishes tidying, gets up with the briefcase in his hand.*) Let's go.

A *consults his watch.*

A: It is now . . . ten . . . twenty-five. We have no train before eleven twenty. Let us kill the time here, talking of this and that.

B: What do you mean, eleven twenty? Ten fifty.

A *takes a time-table from his pocket, opens it at relevant page and hands it to* B.

A: Where it's marked with a cross. (B *consults the time-table, hands it back to* A *and sits down again. Long pause.* A *clears his throat. Pause. Impassionately.*) How many unfortunates would be so still today if they had known in time to what extent they were so! (*Pause.*) Remember Smith?

B: Smith? (*Pause.*) Never knew anyone of that name.

A: Yes you did! A big fat redhair. Always to be seen hanging round World's End. Hadn't done a hand's turn for years. Reputed to have lost his genitals in a shooting accident. His own double-barrel that went off between his legs in a moment of abstraction, just as he was getting set to let fly at a quail.

B: Stranger to me.

A: Well to make a long story short he had his head in the oven when they came to tell him his wife had gone under an ambulance. Hell, say he, I can't miss that, and now he has a steady job in Marks and Spencer's. (*Pause.*) How is Mildred?

B (*disgustedly*): Oh you know— (*Brief burst of birdsong. Pause.*) Good God!

A: Philomel!

B: Oh that put the heart across me!

A: Hsst! (*Low.*) Hark hark! (*Pause. Second brief burst, louder. Pause.*) It's in the room! (*He gets up, moves away on tiptoe.*) Come on, let's have a look.

B: I'm scared!

He gets up none the less and follows cautiously in the wake of A. A *advances on tiptoe upstage right.* B *tiptoes after.*

Theatre II

A (*turning*): Hsst! (*They advance, halt in the corner. A strikes a match, holds it above his head. Pause. Low.*) She's not here. (*He drops the match and crosses the stage on tiptoe followed on tiptoe by B. They pass before the window, halt in the corner upstage left. Match as before. Pause.*) Here she is!

B (*recoiling*): Where?

A *squats. Pause.*

A: Lend me a hand.

B: Let her be! (*A straightens up painfully, clutching to his belly a large birdcage covered with a green silk cloth fringed with beads. He starts to stagger with it towards his table.*) Give it here.

B *helps to carry the cage. Holding it between them they advance warily towards A's table.*

A (*breathing hard*): Hold on a second. (*They halt. Pause.*) Let's go. (*They move on, set down the cage gently on the table. A lifts cautiously the cloth on the side away from the audience, peers. Pause.*) Show a light.

B *takes up the lamp and shines it inside the cage. They peer, stooped. Long pause.*

B: There's one dead.

They peer.

A: Have you a pencil? (B *hands him a long pencil.* A *pokes it between the bars of the cage. Pause.*) Yes.

He withdraws the pencil, puts it in his pocket.

B: Hi!

A *gives him back his pencil. They peer.* A *takes* B's *hand and changes its position.*

A: There.

They peer.

B: Is it the cock or the hen?
A: The hen. See how drab she is.
B (*revolted*): And he goes on singing! (*Pause.*) There's love-birds for you!
A: Lovebirds! (*Guffaw.*) Ah Morvan, you'd be the death of me if I were sufficiently alive! Lovebirds! (*Guffaw.*) Finches, pinhead! Look at that lovely little green rump! And the blue cap! And the white bars! And the gold breast! (*Didactic.*) Note moreover the characteristic warble, there can be no mistaking it. (*Pause.*) Oh you pretty little pet, oh you bonny wee birdie! (*Pause. Glum.*) And to think all that is organic waste! All that splendour!

They peer.

B: They have no seed. (*Pause.*) No water. (*Pointing.*) What's that there?

A: That? (*Pause. Slow, toneless.*) An old cuttle-bone.

B: Cuttle-bone?

A: Cuttle-bone.

He lets the cloth fall back. Pause.

B: Come, Bertrand, don't, there is nothing we can do. (*A takes up the cage and goes with it upstage left. B puts down the lamp and hastens after him.*) Give it here.

A: Leave it, leave it! (*He advances to the corner, followed by B, and puts down the cage where he found it. He straightens up and moves back towards his table, still followed by B. A stops short.*) Will you have done dogging me! Do you want me to jump too? (*Pause. B goes to A's table, takes up briefcase and chair, goes to his table and sits with back to window. He switches on his lamp, switches it off again immediately.*) How end? (*Long pause. A goes to window, strikes a match, holds it high and inspects C's face. The match burns out, he throws it out of window.*) Hi! Take a look at this! (*B does not move. A strikes another match, holds it high and inspects C's face.*) Come on! Quick! (*B does not move. The match burns out, A lets it fall.*) Well I'll be . . .!

A takes out his handkerchief and raises it timidly towards C's face.

(*Translated by the author.*)

Radio I

HE: (*gloomily*): Madam.
SHE: Are you all right? (*Pause.*) You asked me to come.
HE: I ask no one to come here.
SHE: You suffered me to come.
HE: I meet my debts.

Pause.

SHE: I have come to listen.
HE: When you please.

Pause.

SHE: May I squat on this hassock? (*Pause.*) Thank you.
    (*Pause.*) May we have a little heat?
HE: No, Madam.

Pause.

SHE: Is it true the music goes on all the time?
HE: Yes.
SHE: Without cease?
HE: Without cease.
SHE: It's unthinkable! (*Pause.*) And the words too? All the
    time too?
HE: All the time.
SHE: Without cease?
HE: Yes.
SHE: It's unimaginable. (*Pause.*) So you are here all the time?
HE: Without cease.

Pause.

SHE: How troubled you look! (*Pause.*) May one see them?
HE: No, Madam.
SHE: I may not go and see them?
HE: No, Madam.

Pause.

SHE: May we have a little light?
HE: No, Madam.

Pause.

SHE: How cold you are! (*Pause.*) Are these the two knobs?
HE: Yes.
SHE: Just push? (*Pause.*) Is it live? (*Pause.*) I ask you is it live.
HE: No, you must twist. (*Pause.*) To the right.

Click.

MUSIC (*faint*): ....

Silence.

SHE (*astonished*): But there are more than one!
HE: Yes.
SHE: How many?

Pause.

Radio I

HE: To the right, Madam, to the right.

Click.

VOICE (*faint*): . . . .
SHE (*with voice*): Louder!
VOICE (*no louder*): . . . .

Silence.

SHE (*astonished*): But he is alone!
HE: Yes.
SHE: All alone?
HE: When one is alone one is all alone.

Pause.

SHE: What is it like together?

Pause.

HE: To the right, Madam.

Click.

MUSIC (*faint, brief*): . . . .

MUSIC
VOICE (*together*): . . . .

Silence.

SHE: They are not together?
HE: No.
SHE: They cannot see each other?
HE: No.
SHE: Hear each other?
HE: No.
SHE: It's inconceivable!

Pause.

HE: To the right, Madam.

Click.

VOICE (*faint*): ....
SHE (*with* VOICE): Louder!
VOICE (*no louder*): ....

Silence.

SHE: And –(*faint stress*)–*you* like that?
HE: It is a need.
SHE: A need? *That* a need?
HE: It has become a need. (*Pause.*) To the right, Madam.

Click.

MUSIC (*faint*): ....
SHE (*with* MUSIC): Louder!
MUSIC (*no louder*): ....

Radio I

Silence.

SHE: That too? (*Pause.*) That a need too?
HE: It has become a need, Madam.

Pause.

SHE: Are they in the same . . . situation?

Pause.

HE: I don't understand.
SHE: Are they . . . subject to the same . . . conditions?
HE: Yes, Madam.
SHE: For instance? (*Pause.*) For instance?
HE: One cannot describe them, Madam.

Pause.

SHE: Well, I'm obliged to you.
HE: Allow me, this way.

Pause.

SHE: (*a little off*): Is that a Turkoman?
HE (*ditto*): Allow me.
SHE (*a little further off*): How troubled you look! (*Pause.*)
   Well, I'll leave you. (*Pause.*) To your needs.
HE (*ditto*): Goodbye, Madam. (*Pause.*) To the right, Madam,
   that's the garbage—(*faint stress*)—the *house* garbage.
   (*Pause.*) Goodbye, Madam.

Long pause. Sound of curtains violently drawn, first one, then the other, clatter of the heavy rings along the rods. Pause. Faint ping—as sometimes happens—of telephone receiver raised from cradle. Faint sound of dialing. Pause.

HE: Hello . . . Miss . . . is the doctor . . . ah . . . yes . . . he to call me . . . Macgillycuddy . . . Mac—gilly—cuddy . . . right . . . he'll know . . . and Miss . . . Miss! . . . urgent . . . yes! . . . (*shrill*) . . . most urgent!

Pause. Receiver put down with same faint ping. Pause. Click.

MUSIC (*faint*): . . . .
HE (*with* MUSIC): Good God!
MUSIC (*faint*): . . . .

Silence. Pause. Click.

VOICE (*faint*): . . . .
HE (*with* VOICE, *shrill*): Come on! Come on!
VOICE (*faint*): . . . .

Silence.

HE (*low*): What'll I do? (*Pause. Faint ping of receiver raised again. Faint dialing Pause.*) Hello . . . Miss . . . Macgillycuddy . . . Mac—gilly—cuddy . . . right . . . I'm sorry but . . . ah . . . yes . . . of course . . . can't reach him . . . no idea . . . understand . . . right . . . immediately . . . the moment he gets back . . . what? . . . (*shrill*) . . . yes! . . . I told you so! ... most urgent! ... most urgent! (*Pause. Low.*) Slut!

Sound of receiver put down violently. Pause. Click.

MUSIC (*faint, brief*): . . . .

Silence. Click.

VOICE (*faint, brief*): . . . .
HE (*with* VOICE, *shrill*): It's crazy! Like one!
MUSIC (*together*): . . . .
VOICE

Telephone rings. Receiver raised immediately, not more than a second's ring.

HE (*with* MUSIC *and* VOICE): Yes . . . wait . . . (MUSIC *and* VOICE *silent. Very agitated.*) Yes . . . yes . . . no matter . . . what the trouble is? . . . they're ending . . . ENDING . . . this morning . . . what? . . . no! . . . no question! . . . ENDING I tell you . . . nothing what? . . . to be done? . . . I know there's nothing to be done . . . what? . . . no! . . . it's me . . . ME . . . what? . . . I tell you they're ending . . . ENDING . . . I can't stay like that after . . . who? . . . but she's left me . . . ah for God's sake . . . haven't they all left me? . . . did you not know that? . . . all left me . . . sure? . . . of course I'm sure . . . what? . . . in an hour? . . . not before? . . . wait . . . (*low*) . . . there's more . . . they're together . . . TOGETHER . . . yes . . . I don't know . . . like . . . (*hesitation*) . . . one . . . the

[111]

breathing ... I don't know ... (*vehement*) ... no! ...
never! ... meet? ... how could they meet? ... what? ...
what are all alike? ... last what? ... gasps? ... wait ...
don't go yet ... wait! ... (*Pause. Sound of receiver put
down violently. Low.*) Swine!

Pause. Click.

MUSIC   (*failing*): . . . .
MUSIC
VOICE   (*together, failing*): . . . .

Telephone rings. Receiver immediately raised.

HE (*with* MUSIC *and* VOICE): Miss . . . what? . . . (MUSIC
and VOICE *silent*) . . . a confinement? . . . (*long pause*) . . .
two confinements? . . . (*long pause*) . . . one what? . . .
what? . . . breech? . . . what? . . . (*long pause*) . . .
tomorrow noon? . . .

*Long pause. Faint ping as receiver put gently down. Long
pause. Click.*

MUSIC   (*brief, failing*):   . . . .
MUSIC
VOICE   (*together, ending, breaking off together, resuming to-
         gether more and more feebly*): . . . .

Silence. Long pause.

HE (*whisper*): Tomorrow . . . noon . . .

(*Translated by the author.*)

Radio II

Radio II was first performed by the BBC with Harold Pinter (ANIMATOR), Patrick Magee (FOX), and Billie Whitelaw (STENOGRAPHER) in April, 1976. It was directed by Martin Esslin.

ANIMATOR
STENOGRAPHER
FOX
DICK (mute)

A: Ready, Miss?

S: And waiting, Sir.

A: Fresh pad, spare pencils?

S: The lot, Sir.

A: Good shape?

S: Tiptop, Sir.

A: And you, Dick, on your toes? (*Swish of bull's pizzle. Admiringly.*) Wow! Let's hear it land. (*Swish and formidable thud.*) Good. Off with his hood. (*Pause.*) Ravishing face, ravishing! Is it not, Miss?

S: Too true, Sir. We know it by heart and yet the pang is ever new.

A: The gag. (*Pause.*) The blind. (*Pause.*) The plugs. (*Pause.*) Good. (*He thumps on his desk with a cylindrical ruler.*) Fox, open your eyes, readjust them to the light of day and look about you. (*Pause.*) You see, same old team. I hope—

S (*aflutter*): Oh!

A: What is it, Miss? Vermin in the lingerie?

S: He smiled at me!

A: Good omen. (*Faint hope.*) Not the first time by any chance?

S: Heavens no, Sir, what an idea!

A (*disappointed*): I might have known. (*Pause.*) And yet it still affects you?

S: Why yes, Sir, it is so sudden! So radiant! So fleeting!

A: You note it?

S: Oh no, Sir, the words alone. (*Pause.*) Should one note the play of feature too?

A: I don't know, Miss. Depending perhaps.

S: Me you know—

A (*trenchant*): Leave it for the moment. (*Thump with ruler.*) Fox, I hope you have had a refreshing night and will be better inspired today than heretofore. Miss.

S: Sir.

A: Let us hear again the report on yesterday's results, it has somewhat slipped my memory.

S (*reading*): "We the undersigned, assembled under—"

A: Skip.

S (*reading*): ". . . note yet again with pain that these dicta—"

A: Dicta! (*Pause.*) Read on.

S: ". . . with pain that these dicta, like all those communicated to date and by reason of the same deficiencies, are totally inacceptable. The second half in particular is of such—"

A: Skip.

S: ". . . outlook quite hopeless were it not for our conviction—"

A: Skip. (*Pause.*) Well?

S: That is all, Sir.

A: . . . same deficiencies . . . totally inacceptable . . . outlook quite hopeless . . . (*Disgusted.*) Well! (*Pause.*) Well!

S: That is all, Sir. Unless I am to read the exhortations.

A: Read them.

S: ". . . instantly renew our standing exhortations, namely:
1. Kindly to refrain from recording mere animal cries, they serve only to indispose us.
2. Kindly to provide a strictly literal transcript, the meanest syllable has, or may have, its importance.
3. Kindly to ensure full neutralization of the subject when not in session, especially with regard to the gag, its permanence and good repair. Thus rigid enforcement of

the tube-feed, be it per buccam or be it on the other hand per rectum, is *absolutely*"—one word underlined— "essential. The least word let fall in solitude and thereby in danger, as Mauthner has shown, of being no longer needed, *may be it*"—three words underlined.

"4. Kindly—"

A: Enough! (*Sickened.*) Well! (*Pause.*) Well!

S: It is past two, Sir.

A (*roused from his prostration*): It is what?

S: Past two, Sir.

A (*roughly*): Then what are you waiting for? (*Pause. Gently.*) Forgive me, Miss, forgive me, my cup is full. (*Pause.*) Forgive me!

S (*coldly*): Shall I open with yesterday's close?

A: If you would be so good.

S (*reading*): "When I had done soaping the mole, thoroughly rinsing and drying before the embers, what next only out again in the blizzard and put him back in his chamber with his weight of grubs, at that instant his little heart was beating still I swear, ah my God my God." (*She strikes with her pencil on her desk.*) "My God."

Pause.

A: Unbelievable. And there he jibbed, if I remember aright.

S: Yes, Sir, he would say no more.

A: Dick functioned?

S: Let me see . . . Yes, twice.

Pause.

[118]

A: Does not the glare incommode you, Miss, what if we should let down the blind?

S: Thank you, Sir, not on my account, it can never be too warm, never too bright, for me. But, with your permission, I shall shed my overall.

A (*with alacrity*): Please do, Miss, please do. (*Pause.*) Staggering! Staggering! Ah were I but ... forty years younger!

S (*rereading*): "Ah my God my God." (*Blow with pencil.*) "My God."

A: Crabbed youth! No pity! (*Thump with ruler.*) Do you mark me? On! (*Silence.*) Dick! (*Swish and thud of pizzle on flesh. Faint cry from* FOX.) Off record, Miss, remember?

S: Drat it! Where's that eraser?

A: Erase, Miss, erase, we're in trouble enough already. (*Ruler.*) On! (*Silence.*) Dick!

F: Ah yes, that for sure, live I did, no denying, all stones all sides—

A: One moment.

F: —walls no further—

A (*ruler*): Silence! Dick! (*Silence. Musing.*) Live I did . . . (*Pause.*) Has he used that turn before, Miss?

S: To what turn do you allude, Sir?

A: Live I did.

S: Oh yes, Sir, it's a notion crops up now and then. Perhaps not in those precise terms, so far, that I could not say offhand. But allusions to a life, though not common, are not rare.

A: His own life?

S: Yes, Sir, a life all his own.

A (*disappointed*): I might have known. (*Pause.*) What a memory—mine! (*Pause.*) Have you read the Purgatory, Miss, of the divine Florentine?

S: Alas no, Sir, I have merely flipped through the Inferno.

A (*incredulous*): Not read the Purgatory?

S: Alas no, Sir.

A: There all sigh, I was, I was. It's like a knell. Strange, is it not?

S: In what sense, Sir?

A: Why, one would rather have expected, I shall be. No?

S (*with tender condescension*): The creatures! (*Pause.*) It is getting on for three, Sir.

A (*sigh*): Good. Where were we?

S: ". . . walls no further—"

A: Before that, Miss, the house is not on fire.

S: ". . . live I did, no denying, all stones all sides"— inaudible—"walls—"

A (*ruler*): On! (*Silence.*) Dick!

S: Sir.

A (*impatiently*): What is it, Miss, can't you see that old time is aflying?

S: I was going to suggest a touch of kindness, Sir, perhaps just a hint of kindness.

A: So soon? And then? (*Firmly.*) No, Miss, I appreciate your sentiment. But I have my method. Shall I remind you of it? (*Pause. Pleading.*) Don't say no! (*Pause.*) Oh you are an angel! You may sit, Dick. (*Pause.*) In a word, REDUCE the pressure instead of increasing it. (*Lyrical.*) Caress, fount of resipescence! (*Calmer.*) Dick, if you would. (*Swish and thud of pizzle on flesh. Faint cry from* FOX.) Careful, Miss.

S: Have no fear, Sir.

A (*ruler*): . . . walls . . . walls what?

S: "no further," Sir.

A: Right. (*Ruler.*) . . . walls no further . . . (*Ruler.*) On! (*Silence.*) Dick!

F: That for sure, no further, and there gaze, all the way up, all the way down, slow gaze, age upon age, up again, down again, little lichens of my little span, living dead in the stones, and there took to the tunnels. (*Silence. Ruler.*) Oceans too, that too, no denying, I drew near, down the tunnels, blue above, blue ahead, that for sure, and there too, no further, ways end, all ends and farewell, farewell and fall, farewell seasons, till I fare again. (*Silence. Ruler.*) Farewell.

Silence. Ruler. Pause.

A: Dick!

F: That for sure, no denying, no further, down in Spring, up in Fall, or inverse, such summers missed, such winters.

Pause.

A: Nice! Nicely put! Such summers missed! So sibilant! Don't you agree, Miss?

F
S (*together*): Ah that for sure—
Oh me you know—

A: Hsst!

F: —fatigue, what fatigue, my brother inside me, my old twin, ah to be he and he—but no, no no. (*Pause.*) No no. (*Silence. Ruler.*) Me get up, me go on, what a hope, it was he, for hunger. Have yourself opened, Maud would say, opened up, it's nothing, I'll give him suck if he's still alive, ah but no, no no. (*Pause.*) No no.

Silence.

A (*discouraged*): Ah dear.

S: He is weeping, Sir, shall I note it?

A: I really do not know what to advise, Miss.

S: Inasmuch as . . . how shall I say? . . . human trait . . . can one say in English?

A: I have never come across it, Miss, but no doubt.

F: Scrabble scrabble—

A: Silence! (*Pause.*) No holding him!

S: As such . . . I feel . . . perhaps . . . at a pinch . . .

Pause.

A: Are you familiar with the works of Sterne, Miss?

S: Alas no, Sir.

A: I may be quite wrong, but I seem to remember, there somewhere, a tear an angel comes to catch as it falls. Yes, I seem to remember . . . Admittedly he was grandchild to an archbishop. (*Half rueful, half complacent.*) Ah these old spectres from the days of book reviewing, they lie in wait for one at every turn. (*Pause. Suddenly decided.*) Note it, Miss, note it, and come what may. As well for a sheep . . . (*Pause.*) Who is this woman . . . what's the name?

S: Maud. I don't know, Sir, no previous mention of her has been made.

A (*excited*): Are you sure?

S: Positive, Sir. You see, my nanny was a Maud, so that the name would have struck me, had it been pronounced.

Pause.

A: I may be quite wrong, but I somehow have the feeling this is the first time—oh I know it's a far call!—that he has actually . . . *named* anyone. No?

S: That may well be, Sir. To make sure I would have to check through from the beginning. That would take time.

A: Kith and kin?

S: Never a word, Sir. I have been struck by it. Mine play such a part, in my life!

A: And of a sudden, in the same sentence, a woman, with Christian name to boot, and a brother. I ask you!

Pause.

S: That twin, Sir . . .

A: I know, not very convincing.

S (*scandalized*): But it's quite simply impossible! Inside him! *Him*!

A: No no, such things happen, such things happen. Nature, you know . . . (*Faint laugh.*) Fortunately. A world without monsters, just imagine! (*Pause for imagining.*) No, that is not what troubles me. (*Warmly.*) Look you, Miss, what counts is not so much the *thing*, in itself, that would astonish me too. No, it's the word, the notion. The notion brother is not unknown to him! (*Pause.*) But what really matters is this woman—what name did you say?

S: Maud, Sir.

A: Maud!

S: And who is in milk, what is more, or about to be.

A: For mercy's sake! (*Pause.*) How does the passage go again?

S (*rereading*): "Me get up, me go on, what a hope, it was he, for hunger. Have yourself opened, Maud would say, opened up, it's nothing, I'll give him suck if he's still alive, ah but no, no no." (*Pause.*) "No no."

Pause.

A: And then the tear.
S: Exactly, Sir. What I call the human trait.

Pause.

A (*low, with emotion*): Miss.
S: Sir.
A: Can it be we near our goal. (*Pause.*) Oh how bewitching you look when you show your teeth! Ah were I but . . . thirty years younger.
S: It is well after three, Sir.
A (*sigh*): Good. Where he left off. Once more.
S: "Oh but no, no—"
A: *Ah* but no. No?
S: You are quite right, Sir. "Ah but no, no—"
A (*severely*): Have a care, Miss.
S: "Ah but no, no no." (*Pause.*) "No no."
A (*ruler*): On! (*Silence.*) Dick!
S: He has gone off, Sir.
A: Just a shade lighter, Dick. (*Mild thud of pizzle.*) Ah no, you exaggerate, better than that. (*Swish and violent thud. Faint cry from* FOX. *Ruler.*) Ah but no, no no. On!
F (*scream*): Let me out! Peter out in the stones!
A: Ah dear! There he goes again. Peter out in the stones!
S: It's a mercy he's tied.
A (*gently*): Be reasonable, Fox. Stop—you may sit, Dick—

[124]

stop jibbing. It's hard on you, we know. It does not lie entirely with us, we know. You might prattle away to your latest breath and still the one . . . thing remain unsaid that can give you back your darling solitudes, we know. But this much is sure: the more you say the greater your chances. Is that not so, Miss?

S: It stands to reason, Sir.

A (*as to a backward pupil*): Don't ramble! Treat the subject, whatever it is! (*Snivel.*) More variety! (*Snivel.*) Those everlasting wilds may have their charm, but there is nothing there for us, that would astonish me. (*Snivel.*) Those micaceous schists, if you knew the effect (*snivel*) they can have on one, in the long run. (*Snivel.*) And your fauna! Those fodient rodents! (*Snivel.*) You wouldn't have a handkerchief, Miss, you could lend me?

S: Here you are, Sir.

A: Most kind. (*Blows nose abundantly.*) Much obliged.

S: Oh you may keep it, Sir.

A: No no, now I'll be all right. (*To* FOX.) Of course we do not know, any more than you, what exactly it is we are after, what sign or set of words. But since you have failed so far to let it escape you, it is not by harking on the same old themes that you are likely to succeed, that would astonish me.

S: He has gone off again, Sir.

A (*warming to his point*): Someone, perhaps that is what is wanting, someone who once saw you . . . (*abating*) . . . go by. I may be quite wrong, but try, at least try, what do you stand to lose? (*Beside himself.*) Even though it is not true!

S (*shocked*): Oh Sir!

A: A father, a mother, a friend, a . . . Beatrice—no, that is asking too much. Simply someone, anyone, who once saw you . . . go by. (*Pause.*) That woman . . . what's the name?

S: Maud, Sir.

A: That Maud, for example, perhaps you once brushed against each other. Think hard!

S: He has gone off, Sir.

A: Dick!—no, wait. Kiss him, Miss, perhaps that will stir some fibre.

S: Where, Sir?

A: In his heart, in his entrails—or some other part.

S: No, I mean kiss him where, Sir?

A (*angry*): Why on his stinker of a mouth, what do you suppose? (STENOGRAPHER *kisses* FOX. *Howl from* FOX.) Till it bleeds! Kiss it white! (*Howl from* FOX.) Suck his gullet!

Silence.

S: He has fainted away, Sir.

A: Ah . . . perhaps I went too far. (*Pause.*) Perhaps I slipped you too soon.

S: Oh no, Sir, you could not have waited a moment longer, time is up. (*Pause.*) The fault is mine, I did not go about it as I ought.

A: Come, come, Miss! To the marines! (*Pause.*) Up already! (*Pained.*) I chatter too much.

S: Come, come, Sir, don't say that, it is part of your rôle, as animator.

Pause.

A: That tear, Miss, do you remember?

[126]

S: Oh yes, Sir, distinctly.

A (*faint hope*): Not the first time by any chance?

S: Heavens no, Sir, what an idea!

A (*disappointed*): I might have known.

S: Last winter, now I come to think of it, he shed several, do you not remember?

A: Last winter! But, my dear child, I don't remember yesterday, it is down the hatch with love's young dream. Last winter! (*Pause. Low, with emotion.*) Miss.

S (*low*): Sir.

A: That . . . Maud.

Pause.

S (*encouraging*): Yes, Sir.

A: Well . . . you know . . . I may be wrong . . . I wouldn't like to . . . I hardly dare say it . . . but it seems to me that . . . here . . . possibly . . . we have something at last.

S: Would to God, Sir.

A: Particularly with that tear so hard behind. It is not the first, agreed. But in such a context!

S: And the milk, Sir, don't forget the milk.

A: The breast! One can almost see it!

S: Who got her into that condition, there's another question for us.

A: What condition, Miss, I fail to follow you.

S: Someone has fecundated her. (*Pause. Impatient.*) If she is in milk someone must have fecundated her.

A: To be sure!

S: Who?

A (*very excited*): You mean . . .

S: I ask myself.

[127]

Pause.

A: May we have that passage again, Miss?

S: "Have yourself opened, Maud would say, opened—"

A (*delighted*): That frequentative! (*Pause.*) Sorry, Miss.

S: "Have yourself opened, Maud would say, opened up—"

A: Don't skip, Miss, the text in its entirety if you please.

S: I skip nothing, Sir. (*Pause.*) What have I skipped, Sir?

A (*emphatically*): ". . . between two kisses . . ." (*Sarcastic.*) That mere trifle! (*Angry.*) How can we ever hope to get anywhere if you suppress gems of that magnitude?

S: But, Sir, he never said anything of the kind.

A (*angry*): ". . . Maud would say, *between two kisses,* etc." Amend.

S: But, Sir, I—

A: What the devil are you deriding, Miss? My hearing? My memory? My good faith? (*Thunderous.*) Amend!

S (*feebly*): As you will, Sir.

A: Let us hear how it runs now.

S (*tremulous*): "Have yourself opened, Maud would say, between two kisses, opened up, it's nothing, I'll give him suck if he's still alive, ah but no, no no." (*Faint pencil.*) "No no."

Silence.

A: Don't cry, Miss, dry your pretty eyes and smile at me. Tomorrow, who knows, we may be free.